DEDICATIO

This book is dedicated to all of the people who actively seek to better themselves by following a dream and learn that as it unfolds, they are really on a spiritual journey.

Life is such a great proposition!

What Every ^{NEW} Yacht Stewardess Should Know!

Seatrust Yacht Services, LLC

Bloomington, IN  Milton Keynes, UK

authorHOUSE®

AuthorHouse™
1663 Liberty Drive, Suite 200
Bloomington, IN 47403
www.authorhouse.com
Phone: 1-800-839-8640

AuthorHouse™ UK Ltd.
500 Avebury Boulevard
Central Milton Keynes, MK9 2BE
www.authorhouse.co.uk
Phone: 08001974150

First published by AuthorHouse 4/2/2007

ISBN: 978-1-4259-5265-5 (sc)

Printed in the United States of America
Bloomington, Indiana

This book is printed on acid-free paper.

"Once we change our consciousness
of work from self-centered ambition
to
love-centered service,
we begin to experience
the effortless flow
of
divine inspiration."

- Everyday Grace
by Marianne Williamson

TABLE OF CONTENTS

INTRODUCTION

If you are inspired by adventure, motivated by a desire to succeed, and searching for a career that will open countless avenues of opportunity, join the ranks of professional yacht crew.

Congratulations! You love to travel, the sand, the sea, and far corners of the world. You've found a way to make it all happen; you are going to be a crew member on a luxury yacht!

WHO NEEDS THIS GUIDE? HOW CAN YOU EVER SECURE A JOB AS COOL AS THIS?

The precise steps you should take to build a career in this industry are covered later in this book. I would like to encourage you to try yachting and allay any hesitation you may be feeling about venturing into this quest. I want to help you realize that a career as a professional crew member is entirely well within your reach. Here is a quick breakdown of what captains and owners are looking for in their crew members.

Please answer the following questions:
1. Do you enjoy serving and providing for others?
2. Are you enjoyable to be around? Many captains will hire a good attitude over experience any day of the week.
3. Are you reasonably smart, fun, and responsible?
4. Are you ready to travel and make new friends?
5. Are you willing to learn?

If you answered yes to all of these questions, run—don't walk—to your nearest crew agency and set up an interview for representation. They will lead you the rest of the way!

WHAT YOU WILL LEARN FROM THIS GUIDE

The stewardess position is the inside staff entry level position into yachting. This manual is intended to guide you, the new stewardess, through the initial months of your new career. It is a guideline to help you anticipate the demands of your position and acclimate you to onboard living. There is a significant shortage of American stewardesses. If you are between the age of eighteen and forty, you are a prime candidate to join a luxury yacht.

WHAT IS EXPECTED OF YOU AS THE STEWARDESS?

The stewardess manages the interior of the yacht and is in charge of all guest service. The scope of this position is extensive! You will be serving owners and guests, and cleaning, maintaining, and organizing this five-star facility. This includes all surfaces, amenities, carpets, fabrics, service pieces, laundry (other crew members' items as well), appliances, and equipment. Also, you are responsible for organizing all cabinets, holds, lockers, and drawers. You may find yourself engaged in indexing a DVD collection; then taking inventory of all linens, stemware, and silver. You may also be charged with some of the yacht's provisioning—this means buying anything that is needed, from placemats to coffee spoons to comforters to ice buckets. The scope of the stewardess position really is quite involved—that's why you need this book!

The finest qualities you should possess in order to be successful as a yacht stewardess are:
1. Desire to serve others
2. The ability to think ahead
3. The ability to multi-task

The daily tasks on a yacht are extensive and the stewardess' position is dependent upon attention to detail and effective time management. Once you understand the dynamics of cleaning, laundry and guest service, your day will be a coordinated waltz!

WHY YACHTING? THE BENEFITS OF BEING EMPLOYED IN THE INDUSTRY

You are entering an industry unlike any other, and are about to embark on an adventure that will not only allow you to see the world and build self-esteem, but also provide you a means to accumulate enough money to support your home and provide for your retirement. Few jobs allow one to make so much money, travel the world, garner a sense of pride and accomplishment, and live in luxury (although your cabin may be tiny). Even fewer offer to pay for all of one's expenses and provide the ability to keep virtually every penny one earns. You could sell your car, your house, and all of your possessions and live and work on board a yacht! You could free yourself from any reasonable debt in a year and be set to begin anew. There are countless benefits to working on yachts. If you are good at your position and exhibit a good attitude, your success is virtually guaranteed.

Additional immediate benefits of working on these mega-yachts may include extensive worldwide travel and even use of the yacht and the water toys by you, your friends, and family. The owners may extend one of their many homes to you for your vacations, fly you on their private plane, or give you tickets to their private box for a sporting event. Of course, there may also be more boring (but valuable) benefits like 401(k), medical, and dental benefits… they're good too!

As your career in yachting progresses, you may have the opportunity to advance your position and education. Launching your yachting career as a stewardess is simply the beginning. Your desire to explore other interests will likely translate into greater value for the yacht owner. Consider that your passion for cooking may lead you to a chef role. Your love for children may lead you to home-schooling the owners' children, who are onboard for a year-long circumnavigation. Interests in massage therapy, yoga, SCUBA diving, event planning, interior design and beautician skills are in demand on yachts all over the world. Working on a yacht is a terrific avenue to explore and strengthen your specialty. The owner may even pay for your schooling.

WELCOME ABOARD!

Welcome aboard! I'm excited for you, for the future holds unlimited adventure, earning potential, and opportunity for personal exploration. My finest advice to you is to enjoy the process of learning the nature of this unique industry and take pleasure in the people you will meet and the places to which you will travel. While a stewardess holds a position onboard which is essential to a yacht's successful operation, it is unfortunately often the least recognized and appreciated. There is tremendous turnover in this position for this very reason. However, know that once you have demonstrated your skills and a positive attitude, you will become a valuable asset to a savvy owner, captain and a sharp crew-placing agency.

Do your very best. You will be handsomely paid for your effort. Take pride in taking care of and serving others. Delight in the fact that you are running a five star program. If you stick with the career you'll live an exciting and rewarding life on the sea! This is a tough industry. The sacrifices are too great for some. You will be away from home, often with people you do not know, living in a shoebox, and working long hours. That being said, it's also an industry that allows you to tailor your career and accepts a high level of turnover—so leave a boat that does not suit you, if you choose, and find a better one. Your résumé will not suffer in the slightest. But be sure to leave with the best recommendation you can manage, because your reputation is fragile.

If the desire is in your heart to explore this industry, for a season or a lifetime, I encourage you to do so. Enjoy the adventure!

CHAPTER 1

HOW DO THESE BIG YACHTS FUNCTION, ANYWAY?

There are countless private yachts all over the world. Each one functions as a mobile playground for its owner and/or an available charter for any person willing to rent the vessel. There are three primary issues with which an owner and captain are concerned.

1. Safety
2. Maintenance
3. Guest service

Behind the scenes, a well-run yacht has a crew that manages and services the entire yacht and will, at the same time, provide service to owners and guests. These sleek investments can quickly decline in the harsh environment of salt and sea. Thus a well-trained crew is essential to ensure safe operating procedures, meticulous maintenance, and excellent service.

The number of crew members an owner chooses to employ depends on the level of service he expects, as well as the degree to which he would like his vessel maintained. Therefore there is no standard number of crew members employed to run a particular sized yacht. For instance, boats of the length of eighty feet or so may operate with as many as three crew members or with a captain only. Each operation is different.

Temporary crew may be hired for several reasons. If the yacht keeps a fairly frequent travel schedule (two weeks a month), a captain may hire temporary day workers to keep up with maintaining the interior and exterior, while he or she focuses on accounting, planning future trips, and other more specific issues. Larger yachts typically employ enough crew members for every aspect of maintenance and service. However, they too may hire day workers and temporary relief crew to help lighten the load, saving the crew from burnout.

Boats that run without crew are named owner/operator. Occasionally, you will hear of an owner/operator who is looking for a crew member. This means that he's looking for someone to help him enjoy his boat, which may mean that he gets to drive while you do everything else. Ask a lot of questions before you sign on for this kind of job.

POSITIONS ON BOARD CREW MAKE THE WORLD GO ROUND!

Captain: Holds the ultimate responsibility for the safety of the vessel, her passengers and crew. He or she is typically in direct contact with the owner and is in charge of hiring crew, trip scheduling and itinerary, driving the vessel, and keeping up with the general maintenance of the engines and other systems like air conditioning, water makers, electrical, and plumbing—just to name a few!

First mate: Manages all exterior cleaning, waxing, stainless steel, general engine and systems maintenance, and all equipment (such as a tender, davit, and anchor windlass). He or she also assists the captain in driving the vessel and handles lines when docking.

Mate/stewardess: This is a dual role position. He or she is not only the captain's assistant, but is also the manager of the interior of the vessel. For example, when the yacht is underway, the mate/stew will manage docking lines, do engine checks, and assist with driving and navigation. When docked at a marina, he or she will see to all cleaning, laundry, guest service and provisioning for various supplies.

Yachts between eighty and 110 feet may run with as few as two crew members or as many as four. This is simply an estimate; some yachts will run with more crew, some with less. The positions on board may be captain, first mate, chef, and stewardess.

Chef: The chef is hired to provide all of the meal service for crew and guests. The food, beverage, and meal-planning are solely his or her responsibility. Sometimes the chef is expected to assist with lines and fenders when docking.

Steward/Stewardess: The interior of the vessel is the stewardess' focus; this includes laundry, cleaning, stateroom preparation, table setting, bartending, and guest service. Of course, when the vessel is docking, he or she may be expected on deck to manage lines and fenders.

Yachts between 110 and 130 feet may run with four to six crew members—again, depending on the level of personal service and degree of maintenance an owner desires. Beyond what has been outlined above, the additional crew may be:

Engineer: A full-time, onboard engineer is a great addition to a vessel that travels frequently. The engineer is a licensed technician that is capable of keeping all mechanical systems operational. He or she is very handy if you find yourself on the other side of the world with engines that are overheating. On smaller yachts, up to around 130 feet, the position could be mate/engineer, and will obviously bring with it a higher rate of pay.

Deckhand: The deckhand position is an entry level position for exterior staff. He or she is hired to keep the exterior of the yacht clean and orderly.

Second Stewardess: An additional stewardess is a great asset on a larger vessel. Typically, yachts of this size hold four to five staterooms, which can add up to ten guests. If two stewardesses are employed, one may be available for guest service while the other handles the extensive tasks of interior maintenance.

Third Stewardess: The third stew works with the second stew under the direction of the chief stewardess. Many hands make for light work!

Yachts beyond 130 and up to 160 feet will run with between six and twelve crew members. Again this is an estimate. Typically, the positions on board are being doubled up to avoid gaps in service. For example, a first mate will gain help with a bosun and deckhand, and there will be a chief stewardess who will direct the efforts of a second and third stewardess. These six crew members, when accompanied by a captain, chef, and engineer, result in nine crew members.

The yachts that reach up into the 200-foot range operate with more than twenty crew members! So you can see that the potential is here for you to realize a very real career in this industry. These "small cities" cannot operate without you, so go for it!

Think about what a simple day at the beach may require in manpower on a 165-foot yacht. Two crew members go to the beach early to set up the grill, chairs, umbrellas, and coolers. One more gathers the guests and shuttles them out to the beach. The engineer is repairing the water maker, while two stewardesses proceed with cleaning staterooms. The captain attends charting the evening cruise and researching a new port of call the owner would like to visit next month. The chef finishes up in the galley and proceeds to the beach to barbecue lunch, a deckhand attends exterior cleaning, and another stewardess cleans up the breakfast dishes. Hmmmm… how many people is that? The answer is ten! And they may still feel shorthanded and rushed.

Purser: This position is usually found on the large yachts over 150 feet or a busy charter yacht. Basically, the purser works directly under the captain and is in charge of record-keeping, employee benefits, and accounting, as well as all correspondence. He or she is also the liaison between the onboard department heads and the vital link between the vessel and the owner's land-based corporation. The chief stewardess often assumes these duties if there is not someone dedicated to the tasks.

VESSEL POLICIES

Many yachts have crew members who live aboard on a full-time basis. Each boat will have specific policies. While the boat pays for all food and drink for the crew, it may or may not include alcoholic beverages. Some allow smoking, drinking, and even leaving the vessel once guest service is concluded in the evening; but some absolutely do not! You may be able to leave at the end of the day when there are no guests on board, but if the boat is in a boat show, for example, the captain may require crew to stay on board until the end of the show! Trust me, it happens!

Be certain to inquire about the yacht's crew policies so you will know what type of onboard environment you are entering. Otherwise, the sky's the limit in what the yacht may "ask" of you.

PERMANENT VS. FREELANCE—
PLAYING THE FIELD IS A VERY GOOD THING!

The yachting industry is the only one I know that does not hold job-hopping against you. Enjoy this freedom, if it suits you, and hire out as a **freelance stewardess** for a while until you gain some experience. Working in a freelance position means that you are being hired for a specific time - ranging somewhere between one and thirty days. You will then work at a day rate that is typically higher than the daily rate of a salaried position. Current day rates are $125-200, dependent upon experience. Many stewardesses remain freelance stews because the pay is great for the time involved, they can accept or decline a job offer as it suits them, and they are rarely away from their home for too long.

Always do the following before you leave for a freelance job:
1. Confirm your daily rate of pay
2. Confirm you will be paid at least half or all of that rate for your travel days to and from the vessel
3. Confirm that you will be paid upon conclusion of the job before you leave the vessel to return home

While freelance status has its bonuses, there are benefits that may only come while holding a permanent position. These include financial stability, vacation time, medical benefits, a 401(k), cell phones, and even an apartment. If you would like to assess a job for its value to you, use the spreadsheet in chapter 25, *Assessing a Job Offer.*

WHO HIRES FREELANCE STEWARDESSES?

There are a myriad of situations that may arise on a yacht that require the services of a freelance stewardess:
1. Replace a crew member who left unexpectedly
2. Try a freelance person before hiring them permanently
3. Infrequent use of the vessel by the owner, thus a permanent stewardess is not justified
4. Preparation for boat shows, sale, or turn-around after a major refit
5. Extra service required for a trip

If a permanent position is offered to you and you want to take it, know that you can change your mind if you discover that it is not the environment for you. Give proper notice of thirty days to your captain, and move on. Virtually the only thing that can hurt you in this business is a poor attitude or a poor performance report to your crew agent. The industry understands that a good fit for crew and owner can be difficult to make, so do not think that leaving a boat will hurt your career.

Would you rather run a sprint or a marathon? Balancing your workload and free time as a permanent crew member will naturally develop with time as you work out a routine with your fellow crew members and owners. The marathon is pacing yourself so you can provide consistent, quality service with a smile on your face. However, as a freelance stewardess, approaching the job as a sprint is the best approach. This means being very thorough and consistent in your service and always presenting a happy and professional demeanor. A freelance job is an opportunity to impress the captain and the guests. Leave the job a hero!

While away on a freelance job I encourage you to not accept an offer to take a day off (unless you are certain you will be paid for that day anyway) and work straight through for the time that you are on board—mostly because if you are being paid to be away from home, well, be paid to be away from home! As well, as it often happens, a "day off" is rarely ever a day off. Things always come up that seem to require your assistance.

Tip: ⚓

Before you leave the boat, be sure to ask the captain if you can use him as a reference and for a reference letter. The letter can be as simple as a quick email. Print out the letter and keep it with your personal papers. Unfortunately, because you are onboard for such a brief period of time, a captain may not remember you when he is contacted by a potential employer. Thus, maintaining current references is essential. If your reference is two years old, my fear is that their response will be something vague or worse like "I don't remember her stealing anything!"

CHARTER YACHTS VS. PRIVATE YACHTS

If a yacht is run as a private yacht, you can expect it to be used by the owner and his friends only. If the boat charters, you can expect it to be used by different groups who have hired the vessel and her crew, usually for a week or two. Some yachts will do both. They will charter for a certain part of the season, and then return to private use. This helps defray some expenses to the owner, rarely as much as they hope.

Chartering has great rewards for the crew, as it is usually an opportunity to earn extra compensation—for $1,000 is standard gratuity per crew member, per week, while it's not unheard of to receive ten times that! You will, however, have to earn it! Charter guests can be exhausting to a crew because they can be demanding, stay up very late at night (a crew member should be available at all times), and have little, if any, understanding of your job or the length of your day. Back-to-back charters are tough; ten in a row are tougher!

If you find yourself on a yacht that is available for charter, you will need to empty the medicine cabinets, drawers and closets of the owners' belongings so they are available to your paying guests. Use large plastic bags or other liquid-safe containers and store these items away from guest access. There may be specific linens, pillows, and towels dedicated for charter guests, so preparing these items in advance can help you get a jump on preparing the boat for the next cruise.

YACHTS VS MEGA-YACHTS

Here is the only math lesson in this book: the smaller the yacht, the smaller the crew, and the larger the yacht, the larger the crew. Confused? Well, this translates to several tenets:
1. The smaller the crew, the greater the flexibility in the positions, and the greater the opportunity to learn skills beyond your immediate position.
2. An intimate crew setting of a smaller yacht may offer greater liberties, like use of the yacht, her toys, and privacy.
3. Mega-yachts may offer more adventurous travel schedules, overseas crossings, and circumnavigation.

4. Mega-yachts have more crew members, thus more positions and room for advancement. If your dream is to work on a 200-foot yacht, start in an entry-level position of stewardess on as large a yacht as will hire you, and work your way up. You will advance faster than you think, as there is tremendous turn over of crew at the conclusion of each cruising season and your loyalty will be rewarded.

NOTES

_____

_____

_____

_____

_____

_____

_____

_____

_____

_____

_____

_____

_____

_____

_____

_____

_____

_____

_____

_____

_____

CHAPTER 2
HOW TO RESEARCH THE YACHTING INDUSTRY

The best way to familiarize yourself with the yachting industry is by exploring the myriad of websites that cater to the industry. Search for;
1. crew agencies
2. yacht brokers
3. yacht manufacturers
4. boat shows
5. maritime newspapers

The crew agencies offer descriptions and salary guidelines of the different positions on board a yacht, while the newspapers publish articles that are pertinent to captains and crew members. They are your very best resource for gleaning an understanding of the business.

Securing your first job will happen more quickly if you make an effort to meet people in the industry. Attend dock parties, crew socials and maritime events. Often, vendors that attend the boat shows seek temporary workers to prepare for and work during the event. The list is endless in who may enlist your services! You could help a caterer prepare and serve at the parties. Help a broker detail his yachts before the show or serve as a hostess during the boat show. Remember that the broker is selling yachts, yachts that will need crew. By endearing yourself to them you may be recommended to the new owner. The more friends that you make in yachting the more you will learn and the more quickly you will be hired. Yachting is a small community and networking is very profitable.

Tip: ⚓
Prepare business cards with your contact information, nationality, and expertise to hand out to all of the wonderful people you will meet.

NOTES

CHAPTER 3

WHAT TO EXPECT DURING YOUR TIME ON BOARD

THE WORK DAY, THE WORK NIGHT, AND LATE NIGHT

Yachts are vacation play grounds for the wealthy. It is safe to assume that most yachts will be occupied by guests during every holiday and even for some annual events. The good news is you may find yourself at the Super Bowl, The US Open or even the races in Monaco. It is expected that you be available for any of these times and that your vacation time will be scheduled somewhere in between.

Most boats work a five-day-a-week schedule when there are no guests on board. The day might begin at 8:00 AM and wrap up around 4:00 PM. Your weekends are your own, just like a job in the real world. Sometimes they are not. Some yachts invoke a twenty four hour watch onboard. This means that someone will be available around the clock. These shifts are typically rotated between crew members. Confirm the length of the work day and week with the captain, so there are no surprises. When preparing for a trip, all bets are off; you may be required to work straight through the weekend just to ensure the yacht is ready for guests. Some captains are very fair in making up for any days worked over the weekend by offering days off as soon as the schedule permits. Ask about this too.

When owners and guests are on board, all crew members work all day long, into the early evening, and some will work into the wee hours of the morning tending to those late night party guests. A ten-day trip can wear on you like a month's worth of work, because there is simply very little time to rest. Even on the lightest-service yachts, you'll all be busy. The length of the day differs on every yacht. Some owners are generous and release their crew after the evening meal. This allows you to enjoy some free time and stay well rested. Charter guests tend to be less empathetic and have little understanding of the demands of your job. They think nothing of keeping you up all night long. Hopefully, the captain and owner that you work for will be protective of your downtime so that you can remain happy and productive.

Tip: ⚓

Expect to work long hours until you develop an understanding of the yacht's program. Remember, it can be enjoyable, and as outlined in the introduction, very beneficial.

CABIN FEVER It may be small, but you'll find yourself wishing you could spend more time there!

You will be provided a cabin with storage space for your crew uniforms and personal belongings. You can count on a drawer or two and some hanging space. More than likely, you will have a roommate. It is not the least unusual to share your cabin with a member of the opposite sex. This should be disclosed to you in advance, and by all means inquire about the arrangements before you travel.

The bathroom arrangement is different on every yacht. Some dedicate one head for every crew cabin, while others are arranged so that all crew share only one. You will learn as you go which yacht manufacturers thoughtfully plan out the crew quarters and which ones do not. As a crew member you will be provided essential hygiene products; toothpaste, toothbrush, shaving cream, razors, shampoo etc. Any specialty items like make-up, cologne and expensive shampoos should be purchased by you.

YES, THEY EVEN DRESS YOU!

Most yachts will provide you crew T-shirts and shorts to wear while working without guests on board, and a Polo shirt and shorts to wear with guests on board (typically all with the logo of the yacht and the name). You'll be very stylish! Some yachts choose to have crew in more formal attire for the evenings, Sundays, and holidays when guests are on board. This may consist of a skirt or skort, a unique blouse, or even an epaulet shirt.

An important question to ask before joining a boat is exactly what clothing will be provided for you. Don't forget to ask about interior shoes and belts for your uniform. Typically, shoes are not worn inside, but definitely ask! Also, you may want to ask about deck shoes. If they do not provide them, consider buying your own. Deck shoes can save you a lot of pain and possible injury, for there are obstacles on deck on which you can stub your toes and sometimes there are metal posts (for instance, used to secure the boarding ladder or canvas covers) that protrude up from the deck that can puncture your feet. Ouch! Remember, no cussing in front of guests!

LET'S EAT!

Haven't you always wanted a private chef? Have you ever dreamed of eating the finest foods available on Earth? Have you ever imagined the health and vitality (not to mention the body) you would experience if you could dine every meal at a world-class spa? Me too! Yachting is the closest you will come to the experience without it costing you a dime. Typically, the chef will prepare the same food for crew as will be prepared for the guests. It is impressive how lavish some yacht dining experiences can be. You will find yourself enjoying the finest things. Often times too, the chef will cater to specific diets. So if you are vegetarian or high protein, for example, the chef will surely make provisions to accommodate you within reason.

SEASICKNESS

You may not know whether or not you are susceptible to seasickness. That's alright, do not worry about it. There are many solutions beyond medication that can offer some relief. Research it on the Internet. Some crew members suffer from seasickness but manage to enjoy their career anyway. Typically the boat is not in big seas with guests on board so you should not have any trouble doing your job.

Here are some suggestions to help you feel best while at sea. Obviously abstaining from alcohol the night before you get underway will better enable you to endure the boat's motion. Go easy on breakfast and abstain from caffeine the morning of travel too. Ginger is known to calm the stomach. Ginger Ale is effective too. If you find that you are beginning to feel seasick, go outside and breathe in the cool sea air, focus on the horizon. Lying down on the floor in the lowest aftermost spot on the yacht will offer some relief too as that is where there is minimal motion.

NOTES

CHAPTER 4

BEFORE YOU TRAVEL—YOUR PERSONAL AFFAIRS

BILLS & PAY

Making a few preparations before you embark on a freelance job or a circumnavigation around the world can make your time away less stressful. Have your personal bills set up on automatic payment, or entrust someone to handle them for you. There are personal mail services that will accept all of your mail and packages and hold them for you indefinitely. This will cost you about $175 annually.

Your paycheck can usually be automatically deposited into your banking account, so you'll have immediate access to your funds. Many yachts have in-house WiFi that will enable you to remotely access any online accounts you may have. Inquire before you leave for the boat if any of these services are available to crew members. Additionally, many ports of call have Internet cafes.

REST, MY SWEET!

It's always exciting the night before you travel to a new yacht. You may be excited because your career in yachting is beginning and the port of call is a dream. As tempting as it is to go celebrate, know that you won't catch up on your rest once you board, so plan accordingly.

PASSPORTS

Ensure your identification is up to date, and always carry your passport. If you are not a United States citizen, be sure to have the proper papers when entering and exiting the USA. The immigration officials are very strict and will not hesitate to block your entry and send you home. Even simple ID checks are possible as a yacht cruises the coast of the United States. The coast guard can board you at any time, and may board you while you are underway at sea. Make it easy on your captain and have all of your papers with you and in order!

EMERGENCY CONTACT

Virtually all yachts are equipped with satellite communication of some sort, and may include telephone, cellular phone, and Internet service. Obtain the satellite telephone number from the captain and share it with a loved one to use in case they need to reach you.

NOTES

_____

_____

_____

_____

_____

_____

_____

_____

_____

_____

_____

_____

_____

_____

_____

_____

_____

_____

_____

_____

_____

_____

_____

CHAPTER 5

WHAT TO TAKE WITH YOU

Packing your personal belongings for your time on board can be a daunting task! If you are joining a boat in a freelance capacity, my best advice is to imagine you were stranded on a deserted island with only one thing to wear, and take that with you! I say this for three reasons: most yachts will provide you clothing in which to work, space in your cabin space will most likely consist of a drawer or two and about eight inches of closet space (in which to keep these "boat" clothes), and there often isn't an opportunity to go ashore while guests are onboard anyway.

Tip: ⚓
Pack in a soft duffle as rigid cases are difficult to stow.

Cabins can be very, very cold, even if you are in the islands! Take a long-sleeved shirt, socks, and long pants in which to sleep; a T-shirt and shorts, a pair of jeans, and a top. This will get you through most every job, and you have access to the laundry anyway, so you can always wash whatever you need.

If you are joining a yacht as a full-time crew member, you will want to expand your wardrobe a bit and take advantage of all the exciting spots in the many ports of call.

1. Swim suit
2. Sarong
3. Flip-flops
4. Sandals
5. Big straw hat- there is a lot of sun out there!
6. A little black dress, with the perfect bag and heels

Don't forget, there may be some great shopping opportunities, so don't take too much!

GEMS AND JEWELS

Your jewelry will usually be safe on board; take only what you think you might wear, and leave the rest at home. Rings usually get in the way when working in the interior. Your hands are soapy and they slip off, or they catch on the bed frame when tucking in the linens for the custom mattresses. Never wear rings when handling lines! You could lose a finger or be dragged overboard—which is good if you hate the job, but bad if you want to live!

ACCESSORIZE!

1. Sunglasses (of course!)
2. Alarm clock
3. Earplugs (your roommate may snore!)
4. Eye shade (not all cabins have blackout inserts for portholes!)
5. Books, magazines, puzzle books, journal
6. Large beach bag
7. Pedicure tools (buff those calluses; you'll probably be barefoot most of the time!)
8. Camera
9. Laptop
10. Music

MEDICINE

Obviously, you should disclose any critical medical condition to your captain to ensure your own safety. As well, pack the necessary prescriptions to get you through the trip and a bit beyond. There are a number of drugstore chains that will let you fill your prescription in any town, once they have you in their network. Refilling prescriptions overseas, of course, can be entirely different; so take more than you think you may need, if possible. Oh, and always wear clean underwear.

CELL PHONES AND PHONE CARDS—CALL ME!

Cell phones work a mile or two off shore, and some cell services offer roaming in parts of the Bahamas and Mexico. It can cost a fortune, but I would recommend you always take your cell phone with you, just in case. Contact your provider *before* you depart and ask if they service the country to which you are traveling. If they do offer service, they will more than likely have to activate your phone in order for you to be able to access the local system.

My experience is that I can sometimes receive incoming calls, but not place an outgoing one, so tuck that bit of info in your cap. You could arrange in advance for a loved one to call you after you arrive. This way you can test to see if your phone works in the area. Be sure to pack your charger.

Phone cards are a great solution for communicating when traveling abroad, but be sure and be specific regarding from where and to where you will be calling. Also, they tend to expire a year or two after they've been activated, so keep that in mind.

PAPER IS A GIRL'S BEST FRIEND!

If you are working on a commercial vessel—that is, one that is chartering—you will be required by law to have STCW certification. This is the International Convention for the Standards of Training, Certification and Watchkeeping for Seafarers, or the Seafarers Training Certification and Watchkeeper's Code. This is a basic firefighting, water survival, and vessel safety course that ensures your awareness of certain procedures and techniques. The course is usually one week in duration and costs approximately $900. This is not a required course for private vessels. However, it contains very valuable information that could save your life, so do it! Also, many crew agencies will *not* consider you a serious candidate for employment without it, so do it! Lastly, it is a lot of fun if you take it in an area like Ft. Lauderdale, because you will meet many other yacht crew members, and thus have an opportunity to network! So do it!

BE WELL!

You may find that your free time on board is a perfect opportunity to enjoy those interests that you have found it difficult to find time for in the past. I encourage you to take books and DVDs with you on your trip. Explore yoga, meditation, Pilates, a foreign language. Keep a journal or write a book. Take your camera, watercolors or sketch pad and explore your creative side. Living on the water is peaceful and inspiring; I hope you will take advantage of it!

NOTES

_____

_____

_____

_____

_____

_____

_____

_____

_____

_____

_____

_____

_____

_____

_____

_____

_____

_____

_____

_____

_____

_____

_____

CHAPTER 6

YOUR RELATIONSHIP WITH OTHER CREW MEMBERS

SO, YOU WANT TO BE IN A RELATIONSHIP?

Your relationships with your fellow crew members will make or break your time on board, potentially your success in your job, and your reputation in this industry! (No pressure!)

Knowing that people who choose this profession and this way of life are an eccentric bunch, you can hopefully keep your sense of humor while you're learning this new career. So, as a new stewardess; watch, listen, learn, and stay in touch with your humorous side. If not, you can always scream into your pillow at night! That's the best advice I have, because you won't survive otherwise; and hey, the crazier it is, the more information you'll have for *your* book!

Tip: ⚓

Make a commitment to yourself to maintain an even and pleasant personality while living on board a yacht. It is vital that you establish and preserve some level of friendship with each of your fellow crew. This will greatly enhance your experience while onboard and sustain a positive working and living environment. A short-term disagreement can have a long-term impact; it just isn't worth it. Nod and smile, make every effort to see another's viewpoint, maintain the peace to remain at peace yourself.

OH CAPTAIN, MY CAPTAIN!

On a small yacht, you will have a relationship with the captain. Hopefully he or she will take the time to walk you through an orientation of the vessel, outline the specific tasks assigned to you, and supply some insight into the guests' expectations. He may ask you to assist with lines while pulling on and off of the dock, or with launching water toys, etc. This is a great opportunity to learn about yacht systems, navigation, handling, and the myriad of aspects required to keep these small cities functioning. A crew of two to four people will lend itself to someone who desires to learn more than her immediate position. Express an interest, and surely someone will teach you.

WHAT MAKES HER HEAD INDIAN?

The chief stewardess is the queen. When joining a larger vessel that runs with a chief stewardess, you may have little—if any—contact with the captain, and be completely under the supervision of the chief stewardess or steward. As you may recall from a previous chapter, the chief stew is the supervisor of all interior operations. She or he will be highly organized and very specific in explaining your tasks to you. This is really an ideal situation when just starting out in this business, because you simply follow orders. You will learn countless tips and tricks. A week on board with a chief stew can teach you what may take you a year to discover on your own.

SO, THAT CHEF BOYARDEE… IS HE A NICE GUY?

Beyond the relationship you establish with the chief stewardess, the chef is your next most important relationship. You are an integral part of the chef's success. Beyond taking the food to the table for guests, you are the chef's eyes and ears.

You are the chef's liaison to the guests on board. By paying attention to what plans the guests may be discussing, and monitoring the cadence of each meal, you will assist with the timing of food service. For example, if one of the guests has left the table prior to service, inform the chef so that the first course won't be plated and then have to sit in the galley getting warm—or cold, as the case may be! If they've all decided they want to go into town for a bit, and lunch has the possibility of being canceled, inform the chef.

Chefs are unique, and to their credit, they have a very intense job on board a yacht, no matter the size of the vessel. They deal with many obstacles, including cooking for guests and crew, limited storage space for provisions, constant menu changes due to the lack of availability of fresh supplies, special requests, and allergies that were not disclosed by a guest in advance. Additionally, guests change their minds about virtually everything. They can change their minds from no longer dining on board after the chef has defrosted a rack of lamb for twelve, to wanting to now eat at the beach, and the lunch that is currently being prepared doesn't "travel well." Hopefully they will never have to deal with the panic-stricken feeling of finding out the crew has eaten the bananas that were to be that evening's dessert! Always ask if something is available for crew before popping it in your mouth.

Chefs work long hours. They awaken early to prepare fresh muffins and breads. They then move straight into pre-prep for lunch, and then back to custom egg orders for guest breakfast. Lunch is then only a heartbeat away, once the galley is cleared of the morning event. After the lunch service and the galley is cleaned, the chef may begin evening service preparation, including hors d'oeuvres, desserts, and even preparing a marinade for the next day or night. Or he or she may have to go ashore to locate groceries for that evening's meal because the salad greens froze, or simply because the guests' requests for a particular item have been beyond the norm.

So... whew! They have every reason to be intense, but unfortunately it can easily translate to being angry and rude. Just roll with it if you can, say as little as possible, and try to help ease their job. There will be times when you'll think to yourself, "Can't they do anything?" This is a list of things they may or may not ask of you, but I would recommend that you assume you will be doing them.

1. Empty the dishwasher
2. Stow all dishes
3. Retrieve all china for each course of the meal service
4. Retrieve all platters for meal service, i.e. hors d'oeuvre tray
5. Hand-wash the china and silver
6. Remove the garbage
7. Assist with galley cleaning at the conclusion of the day

FIRST MATES, BOSUNS, ENGINEERS, AND DECKHANDS... WE HAVE OURSELVES A FAMILY!

Your working relationship with the outside crew will be minimal on a large vessel, because there will be deckhands who are dedicated to handling lines, fenders, and water toys. They may not need you, but always offer your help, because it's really quite fun being part of the operation. You'll witness firsthand the coordinated effort of docking a mega yacht. Plus, you may learn you like it out there, and you may choose to pursue a deck/stew position in the future or a deck position singularly. The industry offers many combinations of employment!

The mates and deckhands are usually a great group—friendly and fun! They will welcome any interest in learning you may convey, and will always appreciate any help you offer them. Ask often! You may even learn how to operate a davit, which lowers a tender or Jet Ski into the water. These are such cool things to know.

So while working outside may be an option on a large yacht, typically a smaller vessel running with only four or five crew may require your help in certain situations. The stewardess and the chef may be asked to handle lines when pulling on and off of the dock. The first mate and deckhand (if any) will be on deck and will instruct you.

Tip: ⚓

The most effective way to throw the line to the dock is to gather the majority of it loosely in your dominant hand, a loop or two in the other, and throw with a side arm motion like a discus thrower in the Olympics! Start with the line low and behind you, your body slightly turned away from your target. Then rotate forward, releasing the line with your arm so that your arm just finishes under shoulder height of the opposite arm. This is really helpful when casting heavy lines long distances! Remember your goal is to throw the line slightly beyond the person on the dock, not perfectly to them.

Tip: ⚓

Fenders are inflatable cushions that hang from the railing and are used to protect the hull. They are positioned between the hull and the pilings and/or the dock to protect the dock...just kidding, they protect the boat. They are not called 'bumpers', 'squishy things' or anything else.....not by anyone cool anyway.

NOTES

CHAPTER 7

YOUR DAY VS. THEIR DAY

	THEM	YOU
0600	Dreaming of bonbons, ice cream, and truffles!	Bathing—we hope! Starting the coffee Setting the table
0800	Bathing in their Jacuzzi tub	Cleaning the interior
1000	Deciding whether to add truffles or	Turning over the crabmeat to their omelet laundry Setting the table
1200	Sunning themselves and	Trying to change the vacuum bag Jet Skiing
1400	Ashore for shopping	Drying the beach towels Scrubbing the heads
1600	Munching on hors d'oeuvres	Mixing cocktails Setting the table
1800	Eating lobster al fresco	Gulping down lobster between serving courses
2000	Martinis for everyone!	Turning down the beds Drying the wine glasses
2200	Watching a movie	Ironing the napkins Mopping the galley
2400	Asking for munchies	Restocking the drink refrigerators on deck
0200	Returning from a night at the casino	Cleaning the salon

The point is, you are not a guest, and it may very well depress you the first time you feel it. I'm sorry! But I assure you that if you commit to being an exceptional stewardess, a hard worker, a mature and happy coworker, your career has no boundaries. You will be in the heart of the most luxurious lifestyle in the world. Imagine the clientele, the mega yachts, the private estates, the world wide travel. These clients want and need exceptional people on their team. Once you develop a rhythm in your job, it will in a way become a playful game. Set your sights beyond where you begin. Find the fortitude to endure, the vision to persevere and the willingness to succeed. It will get easier and more profitable as you go and your free time will be spent in some of the most exotic places in the world!

NOTES

_____

_____

_____

_____

_____

_____

_____

_____

_____

_____

_____

_____

_____

_____

_____

_____

_____

CHAPTER 8

YOUR FOCUS AS SOON AS YOU BOARD—boarding the same day as your guests.

If you have the luxury of learning the boat over a few days or weeks, you can take your time and do these things listed here. If you have less than a whole day, tackle this list and you will be well-oriented to do a great job.

First, inquire about the events planned for the day or evening, so that you may prioritize your tasks and have this information to mull over while you take a quick spin through the vessel.

A. *Walk*—Take a walk through the boat and open every cabinet, closet, and drawer. Just take a look, so at least you've seen everything on board.

B. *Chill*—Check the refrigerators inside and on deck, and ensure that they are clean. Cans occasionally explode after being subjected to the motion of the boat. Also check that there is a nice selection of cold drinks, arranged with labels facing out. Chill several bottles of {white} wine for dinner.

C. *Bar*—Take a quick look for the most popular liquors; vodka, scotch, rum, gin, and any mixers and garnishes—for example, soda, tonic, or cranberry juice; and olives, onions, and cherries.

Tip: ⚓
The refrigerator in the galley is almost never used for beverages—there just isn't any room!

D. *Staterooms*—Inspect each stateroom and head to ensure that they are clean, well supplied, the light bulbs are all functioning, and the beds are made. This way, evening turndowns will hold fewer surprises.

E. *Wine & Dine*—Inventory the glasses, plates, and silver flatware so that you will know if you have enough pieces to see you through meal service. For instance, this will help you determine whether you will need to wash the forks from the first course so they will be available to use for the dessert course.

F. *Inspect*—Choose your placemats and napkins for the meal to ensure you have the right quantity and they are clean and pressed.

G. *Meds*—Inventory the medicine box and place one of the small vials of motion sickness pills in your pocket or in a drawer where you can quickly access it. It happens very, very often that a guest boards, and when feeling the slightest queasiness, will ask for medicine from you. You may as well have it on you, because you'll inevitably be focused on some other urgent task when the request comes.

NOTES

_____

_____

_____

_____

_____

_____

_____

_____

_____

_____

_____

_____

_____

_____

_____

_____

CHAPTER 9

YOUR TASKS ONE-BY-ONE

YOUR NUMBER ONE GOAL—Service

All crew are hired to facilitate the owner's use of their yacht. While every owner is different in his or her needs and desires, typically, service will be your primary task, while interior maintenance is second. Time will reveal their habits, likes, and dislikes, and you will breeze right through once you learn them, if you are paying attention. It is very important for you to be consistent in the following:

1. Your level of service—a decline in service is more noticeable than a steady increase. Relate it to an enjoyable night out for dinner with friends, and then having to track down the server for your bill!
2. How you prepare the staterooms
3. How you set the atmosphere of the vessel—lighting, music, and flowers
4. Try to do the same things at the same time of each day—meal service, turndowns, and nuts on the bar!

Consistency in service is a definite endurance test; it's easy to get sloppy, lazy, and forgetful, especially if you are tired. So, what is great service?

"GREAT SERVICE IS LIKE ROMANCE"

I define great service like some define romance—meeting a need or desire before it is expressed. For example, if a guest takes hot tea after dinner for the first two nights of your trip, simply brew it and deliver it to them on subsequent nights. This way, you avoid unnecessary interruptions, and too, the guest can always choose not to drink it! This is thoughtful service, and has the added benefit of being easier on you! Thinking ahead lets you take care of a 'request' before it occurs and when *you* have a free moment. It also helps avoid the feeling of always playing "catch-up."

CAN WE TALK?

Communicating with the host or hostess is the surest way to get any information you need to ensure smooth service. Keep your questions direct and to the point, and they will not mind the interruption. By keeping your eye on the hostess, a moment will probably present itself to steal a second of her time. Remember, you are an extension of the chef, so setting a time for a meal or asking if being seated in, say, thirty minutes is agreeable will keep the galley service in sync. As well, you can properly time pouring the ice water into the glasses on a 102-degree day!

WHAT YOUR GUESTS THINK THEY KNOW!

They think you work, eat, and sleep in luxury, just like they do.

They think you have a limitless amount of space to store any item they may desire.

They think you have a limitless amount of energy to accomplish your job.

They think you are available twenty-four hours a day without a break.

The reality is, in a way, they are right. What they never seem to know is how hard you are working—nor should they! Keep your own counsel; never complain in front of a guest. It is easy to become jaded when your guests are not courteous to you or are overly demanding of you. Do your best to remember that great service is your job, the very reason that you were hired. Always deal with guests courteously, for this is the foundation of exceptional hospitality. If you encounter genuine problems, notify your captain.

I HAVE NEEDS, DEAR!

Preference sheets for guests are a fantastic way to know in advance what your guests will expect while on board. These sheets should be filled out in advance of a trip, and can include anything the captain and crew need to know to facilitate their enjoyment. These are critical for charter guests, as you will learn a great deal about them and be better prepared for their visit.

Consider creating your own preference sheet and asking the following:

1. How many guests will be in your party? Children? Ages?
2. Will you be celebrating a special occasion while on board?
3. What activities interest you the most? Sunning? Beach? Shopping? Movies?
4. Do any guests suffer from allergies or allergic reactions?
5. Have you chartered a yacht before? What was your favorite memory from the trip?
6. Will you need dinner reservations? Limousines? Concert tickets while in New York?

GUEST HOSPITALITY

How you relate to the guests will affect their impression of your service. Keeping notes as you go on guests' preferences will greatly enhance your service and save you time, not to mention impress them. And, if they will be visiting again in the future, you can refresh your memory and provision for that unique tea they love, or offer them their favorite libation before they've even requested it. You might say, "Mr. Soandso, I recall you enjoy a Gibson up, would you care for one this evening?" Notes also make it easier to anticipate repeat requests and take care of them in advance. Why? Because you can execute when you have a moment to do so, and not be interrupted when you're bound to want to focus on another task. For instance, to simply deliver a guest an orange juice in the morning if they've enjoyed it for two mornings in a row is quicker for you than if they have to ask for it. They can always say "no, thank you" or just not drink it. It is no big deal.

You will be in charge of replenishing beverages in the bar and deck refrigerators, chilling wine and champagne for the day, and setting out nuts and nibbles as you see fit. I think two hours after lunch is a good time. It shows you're thinking about them.

CLEANING & MAINTAINING THE INTERIOR—The slow and steady decline!

Before guests board, you should clean and organize the interior as thoroughly as possible, because once they arrive, it tends to be a slow and steady decline. I suggest you do the following to ensure you have as smooth a cruise as possible:

1. Clean all staterooms and heads.
2. Clean and stock all beverage refrigerators—all labels facing out, please!
3. Replace the vacuum cleaner bag.
4. Fill all salt and pepper shakers—ensure the holes are large enough for the grains!
5. Fill all tissue boxes—create a flower by removing several sheets and joining the corners together by folding up from the center. Replace all of the sheets in the opening of the tissue box and fan.
6. Fill all liquid hand soap dispensers.
7. Place a fresh full roll of toilet paper in each head and fold. The paper should feed from the top of the roll.

Tip: ⚓

To fold toilet paper, begin from the end of the roll, fold the corners toward the middle, making a point. Fold the point up the roll, creasing at the base of the triangle. It now looks like a triangle with the point at the top. Now fold the whole piece up once more by grasping the bottom edge and enclosing the triangle completely. This should have created a rectangle with the triangle underneath. Now, fold down the two top corners, bringing them together creating a point that is pointing up. Finally, grasp the point at the top and unfold one time.

If you choose to be more elaborate, use the pocket that has been formed to hold a separate square of tissue folded in a fan shape. Detach one square of tissue before you fold the toilet paper. Lay the tissue on a flat surface. Beginning from the bottom edge, fold the tissue away from you, over a quarter of an inch and crease. Flip the whole piece over, maintaining your grasp. Now, fold the folded piece toward you one quarter of an inch. Flip the whole piece over and repeat until the entire piece is folded. Fold the ends toward each other creasing in the middle. Grasp the middle and fan out the edges. Tuck the folded edge into the pocket that is formed on the toilet paper roll.

8. Clean the lint screens of all of the clothes dryers (they can be filled with sand from a previous trip).
9. Fill the serving piece that holds sweeteners and the sugar bowl.
10. Clean all interior windows.
11. Clean all the surfaces in the pilot house.
12. Clean all the surfaces of the salon, lounge, and day head.
13. Plump up all of the sofa and chair cushions and straighten the décor.
14. Dispose of all extra cartons, boxes, and garbage.
15. Stock the bar and cut the fruit.

Guest Staterooms — these should be serviced a minimum of two times daily when guests are on board.

Before guests arrive:

1. Make the beds (iron the top portion of the bottom and top sheets while the bed is made).
2. Wipe clean the drawers, the telephone, and the light bulbs.
3. Vacuum the carpet, the soft wall panels, and even the ceiling where the air conditioning is vented.
4. Wipe down all surfaces.
5. Check that all outlets and light bulbs are functioning.
6. Ensure drawers are empty and ready for guests' belongings.
7. Soldier the hangers in the closet (use your fingers to create equal spacing between them on the bar).

Tip: ⚓
Felt strips and discs with sticky backs are sold on sheets of paper in different craft and hardware stores. These can be placed on the arms of hangers to

prevent silky garments from sliding off or taped under objects (like a wine bottle coaster) to prevent them from scratching wooden surfaces.

<u>Guest bathrooms</u>—detailing the heads can be tough, because there are so many reflective surfaces. Smears are relentless and almost always obvious. The moment you think the head is clean; I suggest you sit on the toilet to gaze at the mirror and other shiny surfaces to check for sure! This is when your guest is most likely to notice anything.

1. Put out fresh toilet paper (give the remaining roll to crew).
2. Put out a set of towels for each guest in the room, folding them in creative ways.
3. Ensure the vanity supplies are filled (toothpaste, shampoo, and aspirin).
4. Wipe the floor down with disinfectant and paper towels.
5. Wipe the toilet seat with disinfectant and paper towels.
6. Check that hot and cold water is available in the shower and sink.
7. Check that the exhaust fan is clean and working.
8. Check that the medicine cabinet and shower doors open easily. They tend to shift after time, as the motion of the boat can tweak the hinges.
9. Check for good water pressure.
10. Use a toilet brush in the head with a detergent, or a combination black water tank treatment and cleaner.
11. Stock the head with extra supplies like toilet paper, tissues, and soap.

Ethics, please! Do not wipe the handles for the tap with the paper towel you just used to wipe dry the toilet seat!

Tip: ⚓
You can wrap the toilet paper in a pretty tissue or store it in an attractive box to preserve it and keep it clean.

Tip: ⚓
Once guests have departed, it is vital to flush each head two or three times in order to move any product through the pipes and into the black water tank.

If the head sits idle with product in the hopper or the pipes, an enormous stench will develop and take a great deal of time and effort to remove.

Cleaning Products—exercise great care in choosing cleaning products. You are likely to find a myriad of surfaces in the interior of a yacht: leather, suede, marble, granite, glass, mirror, stainless steel, gold, silver, acrylic, Lexan, and wood. Err on the side of caution. Most yachts use very simple products that yield great results without harming delicate finishes.

Marble and wood:	a few drops of Ivory soap in water in a spray bottle
Glass:	a solution of vinegar and water
Gold and silver:	water with a smooth diaper rag

Tip: ⚓
Apply a water repellant product to glass shower doors to prevent spotting. This also makes it quick and easy to dry after each use.

Tip: ⚓
Marble is very porous and will become etched if you spray it with vinegar and water. It is usually sealed and polished to repel liquids. However, it will stain if water or other solutions are allowed to sit on it for too long. Granite is a harder surface and less vulnerable.

Cleaning Equipment—some things to consider for the interior beyond the expected

Squeegees for bathrooms

Chamois for quick drying

Diaper rags for delicate surfaces and lint-free cleaning

Lint roller to pick up loose hair on pillowcases, sheets, and lint up off the bathroom rug

Tip: ⚓
Use a chamois mop, as is used on deck, for mopping the floors and for dusting difficult to reach areas, like the dashboard in the pilot house.

Maintaining the Interior

The following is a list of products you may want to consider for protecting and maintaining the interior:

1. Sticky, pliable putty to secure objects temporarily to surfaces.
2. Felt strips to keep objects from scratching wooden surfaces.
3. Rubber disks placed strategically on surfaces where doors and drawers, when opened, may collide.
4. Touch-up pens to disguise scratches in wooden surfaces.
5. Silver polish.

While guests are on board, constant straightening and attention may be required to maintain the salon, the outer deck spaces, and sky lounge. Try to vacuum and tend to any major cleaning when guests are off of the boat, especially if it requires you to climb up on the furniture! Also, do not be tempted to toss the day's newspaper; invariably someone will later want to read it.

ORGANIZING THE PROVISIONS

You will be in charge of organizing and stowing certain provisions on board. This will include beer, wine, sodas, liquor, mixers, bottled water, drink garnishes, bar nuts and nibbles, cleaning supplies, napkins, placemats, tablecloths, napkin rings, china, silver, crystal, linens, soap, toilet paper, and other head supplies. **Basically, if it's outside of the galley, you need to know where it is, where it goes, and where to find more to replace it.**

Storage spaces are located underneath sofas, mattresses, banquettes, and behind paneled walls. Use your imagination, and use the storage spaces wisely. You can purchase plastic bins to keep things reasonably fresh and dry. Consider storing items like wine, beer, and soda in the lower, cooler parts of the boat, so they will not be subjected to too much motion. Things that will not perish, like extra laundry soap, can be stowed in the bilges.

EXTRA PROVISIONS

You may want to consider furnishing the vessel with some or all of the following:

1. Balloons, ribbons, and party supplies
2. Current magazines—especially the gossip ones people rarely buy but love to read!
3. Monogrammed stationery for each cabin
4. Soft throws for the sofa or beds
5. Pillows of both down and an alternative
6. A bound manual in each stateroom explaining the operation of the audio visual system, out lining special features of the room, safety procedures, interesting specifications of the yacht and even crew member biographies!
7. Candles—there are realistic, battery-operated candles and votives that are lovely and safe

PREPARING THE VESSEL FOR GUESTS

It requires a great deal of hard work to prepare a vessel for guests. The following is not a comprehensive list of what to do before they arrive, but it will give you an idea where to begin.

1. Clean and prepare all staterooms.
2. Clean and prepare all bathrooms (heads).
3. Clean all interior windows.
4. Clean all interior surfaces.
5. Clean all air conditioning filters.
6. Clean, organize, and stock all refrigerators.
7. Inventory wine, liquor, and beverage stock.
8. Prepare all items used in service (silver, crystal, napkins, tablecloths, and serving trays).
9. Prepare exterior areas (rolled towels, clean cushions, atomizers, and lotions).
10. Check all interior lighting.
11. Be prepared to store large pieces of luggage—plastic garbage bags can protect it, should it be stowed in an exterior locker.
12. Set up a basket with snacks and candy for guests' enjoyment.

Tip: ⚓

Set up a basket on the vanity with luxury miniature products for your guests to enjoy. These may include:

Shampoo
Conditioner
Bathing salts
Salt scrubs
Loofah
Shaving cream
Deodorant
Toothbrush
Toothpaste
Dental floss
Mouthwash
Headache medicine
Sun block
Sewing kit
Lint roller
Hairdryer
Scissors (Remember that your guests are on vacation; typically they arrive with tags on new clothes!)

Tip: ⚓

Providing fun products creates added value for very little expense. You could provide a spa package of sea salt scrub, body buff puffs, lip and eye creams, fragrances, and atomizers. All of these can be ordered with custom labels to help celebrate a special event, say Cooper and Buffy's first million!

Tip: ⚓

Purchase large bottles of shampoos, body wash, and hair conditioners, so you can refill the miniatures you have in each stateroom for your next group of guests.

<u>Day of Arrival</u>—The day that guests arrive on board is always a very busy time, mostly because some aspects of preparation can only be done at the last minute. This may include:

1. Setting out exterior deck cushions, rolled towels, and sun block
2. Pulling up the carpet runners
3. Making one more dusting pass
4. Setting out the flowers
5. Setting out highly breakable *objets d'art*
6. Setting out a shoe basket and chair on the dock to welcome guests to the yacht
7. Chilling wine, setting the table, and pulling service pieces for the chef
8. Staging the interior with music and lighting

Don't forget to reserve some time for yourself to get cleaned up and changed into your uniform.

Atmosphere—while maintaining cleanliness and order is certainly a priority as the trip progresses, it is also critical to create a welcoming atmosphere at all times.

1. If it's dark and overcast outside, it's probably very dark below deck in the cabins. Pop down and set some mood lighting!
2. Set out a basket of nicely rolled beach towels.
3. Set out a basket with a selection of sun block, creams, atomizers, and lip balm.
4. Welcome new guests with iced champagne.
5. Set out small food on which to nibble (nuts, wasabi peas, mini sweet pickles, olives).
6. Chocolate, available at all times, is of course always a nice touch!

SETTING THE TABLE

Preparing for each course is a must. Begin by discussing the menu with the chef and ask what style dish and what silverware they would like to use for each course. They have an image in mind for their presentation. For instance, a course may be saucy and require a soup-style bowl.

Basic table setting is fork on the left, knife on the right, and any additional utensils for courses preceding the main course are set on the outside of these. Diners will work their way toward the plate as they use the flatware for each course. It's really very logical! Think of how the utensil is utilized, and it will give you a clue how to place it. For instance, the knife blade faces in toward the plate, because as you pick it up to cut your food, it will be in the most effective orientation—sharp side down, for all of you remedial thinkers out there! The soup spoon is placed on the right, next to the knife. Can you imagine why? Because most diners are right-handed, and the soup will be served before the knife may be required. Dessert utensils are placed at the top of the plate, with the fork tines pointing toward the right and the spoon pointing toward the left. If both a fork and spoon are set for the dessert course, the fork is placed below the spoon.

Chargers are large, decorative plates placed on the table for each diner. Service plates are placed on top of the charger for all courses except the dessert course. Butter plates are placed to the left of each place setting, with a butter knife if available. Remove the butter plates at the conclusion of the main course, before the dessert course is served. Chargers and butter plates may or may not be used. Remember, you are on a boat. Storage space is often limited, and tables are often small and oddly shaped, so there may not be room to set a complete and proper table.

If you will be serving coffee and tea after dinner, be sure to place the cups, saucers, cream, and sugar pieces in the galley or a place where you can access them quickly. Often they are stowed in the dining room and retrieving them once the meal begins can be difficult and embarrassing.

EXTRAS!

Salt and pepper are a given, but there may be condiments that will be served that may require small dishes and serving spoons. Additionally, there may be a need for an extra dish on the table—for example, a bowl that the guests may use to place empty seafood shells that they want to set aside, off of their plates. It is helpful to ask yourself what you might want if you were the diner as you think through the stages of any meal.

Tip: ⚓

Condiments are more inviting when placed on a plate with a lace doily underneath.

Tip: ⚓

Butter can be formed into attractive shapes by softening it to room temperature and then spreading it into a mold. You also can simply cut it into shingles and arrange them decoratively on a plate with a garnish in the middle.

WHAT'S YOUR THEME?

Using a theme to guide you in table decoration is a great way to set a mood and provide new interest for guests. Your theme can be centered on the food that will be served or something else entirely! I've seen countless themes: an African safari where lions, tigers, and elephant figures were paired with masks and animal prints; or tables where figurines of obese sunbathers, etc. were paired with bright pink sunglasses and mini umbrellas to create a "tourist beach" theme! There are a lot of tchotchkies in the world. Doesn't it make you feel good, knowing they won't go to waste? Remember, unique days like St. Patrick's Day and April Fool's Day can be great inspiration. So can the current popular movie. Have fun with it.

CENTERPIECES

Typically, flower arrangements will be ordered prior to guest arrival. You can certainly use these as your centerpiece for meals. Tips on placing orders for flowers and flower arranging are expanded later in this chapter under *Purchasing*. If however, it's too windy to place flowers on the aft deck table, they have lost their elegance during the trip, or you simply want to provide some variety, consider other items you may have on hand. Even a large compote filled with lemons and limes is a bright and fresh solution for a breakfast or lunch table. You can also take simple items like chopsticks and bamboo mats and group them with some dried grasses to create an Asian theme. Provided it doesn't send your guests into Vietnam flashbacks, it's a cute idea!

Tip: ⚓

Yachting and interior decorating magazines are great resources for table setting ideas.

NAPKINS

Cloth napkins are preferred over paper napkins on most yachts. Keep in mind that cloth will need to be ironed after washing. When setting the table with cloth napkins, you have several options.

Napkin rings are a quick solution, provide variety, and can keep the wind from carrying the napkin off into the deep blue sea! You can find inexpensive ones, and even make them yourself if you are creative. Choose your rings wisely! Remember that they will be in a saltwater environment, and anything that is metal may rust or corrode. There are many materials available that will endure the saltwater environment— glass, plastic, wood, and glass beads are all durable.

Otherwise, napkin folds are an interesting alternative, and illustrative books are available to learn this skill. Most yachts will have one or two on board. The following are some very simple instructions for three napkin folds. You will have the best success with a stiff, square napkin, not a synthetic flimsy one.

Tip: ⚓

Choose your napkins wisely! Be sure they will wash and wear well. When partially made with synthetic material, they require less ironing and stain less easily. This reminds me, do not use your finest linen napkins when foods like butter laden lobster or beets will be served, they will be irreparable!

Envelope: Place the square napkin in front of you. Bring the top corners to the bottom corners by creasing in the middle. You should have a rectangle. Take the left side of the napkin over to the right side of the napkin, creasing in the middle, forming a square. Working from the right side, bring the upper and lower corners of the top layer toward each other until they meet, forming a point. Lift this top layer by the point and fold it to the left, creasing so the point slightly overhangs the very left side. Working from the right side again, bring the corners of the bottom layer toward each other until they meet, forming another point. Lift this bottom layer by the point and fold it to the left, creasing so the point lies inside the first triangle. You should have an envelope shape with a double flap.

Triangle: Place the square napkin in front of you. Bring the top corners to the bottom corners by creasing in the middle. You should have a rectangle. Fold the top corners toward the middle, meeting at the bottom. You should now have a triangle. Fold the outside corners together creating one single triangle. Stand up on the longest side.

Flower: Place the square napkin in front of you. Bring all four corners to the middle. Again, bring all four corners to the middle. Supporting the middle with one hand, gently flip over the napkin. One more time, fold all four corners to the middle. While holding the corners securely in the middle, reach under each corner that you just brought in, and gently pull out the corner that is lying beneath. This will form a petal of sorts in which you can place a seashell, a dinner roll, or a tiny wrapped gift. This napkin fold can also be used to frame a soup bowl.

SERVING THE MEALS

Prior to Service ~ to begin table service, pour the water just *before* the guests are seated. Follow with the wine immediately *after* they are seated and with the bread by tongs immediately after that. To minimize interruption, do not ask if they want wine or bread, simply serve it. If they do not want to be tempted, they will either say something to you or offer it to someone else at the table.

The Order of Service ~ place each course by serving the guest of honor first, if any, or the hostess, then every other lady at the table in counterclockwise fashion, then all of the men, and then the host. The order of service is debatable among people—and countries, for that matter! It is proper to serve the hostess first, though some hostesses are embarrassed by this ritual. I have witnessed hostesses actually pass their plate over to someone else. I prefer to serve her first so that she can lead the rest of the diners. When she begins eating, the others may begin eating. Also, she sets an example.

My aunt was dining formally one evening as a young adult in a home in Europe. After the entrée had been cleared, the server began circling the table with linen draped over his arm and a tray, upon which sat a swan statue carved in ice encircled with beautiful pieces of fruit. Well, each of the young girls, when presented the tray, chose a piece of fruit. When the hostess was presented with the tray, however, she simply stroked her fingertips across the swan and promptly dried them on the linen draped over the server's arm! The fruit was simply decoration. Now, imagine—had she led this ritual, her guests would have been spared untold embarrassment!

Remember you can always ask your hostess what order she would prefer you to serve, and then you will have one less thing about which to concern yourself.

Serving and clearing ~ Provided there is space available around the table and you are able to reach each guest, serve from the left and clear from the right. Why? This custom stems from more formal service in the past. As the hired helped circled the table, they greeted each diner with a platter of food on which was placed serving utensils. Having the platter presented on the diner's left side was conducive to serving oneself (if the diner was right handed). Sorry left handers! Imagine how much more comfortable it is to reach across the front of your body to serve your plate then it would be to be cramped while trying to serve yourself from a platter presented on your right side. Water, wine and other beverages are poured from the right. Why? Well, that is where the glass is. Reaching across a diner is disruptive and inappropriate.

Clearing from the diner's right is a custom that stems from the placement of silverware at the conclusion of the meal. The diner *should* place the handle of both the knife and fork together at the four o'clock position on the plate. When you remove the plate, lay your thumb over the utensils to keep them from sliding off of the plate.

Clearing the table as guests finish a course is something about which you will have to make a personal judgment. Should you wait until everyone at the table has finished? Should you clear plates as soon as they are empty? Obviously, if a diner has pushed his plate away from him toward the center of the table, he wants you to take it away!

Waiting until at least half of the diners have finished before beginning to clear is a nice rule of thumb. Then *slowly* begin removing two plates at a time (from the diner's right), being certain <u>not to leave only one person eating</u> while all of the others have been cleared. Consider leaving the plates on either side of a guest who is still eating. This way, the last diner will not feel as rushed to finish.

Tip: ⚓
<u>Never stack plates or scrape food onto other plates</u> at the table or in the view of guests. This behavior is atrocious and completely unacceptable.

The chef may serve the meal in a variety of ways. She may serve via a buffet, family-style (where dishes are passed around the table and guests serve themselves), or plate each course individually in the galley and have you serve the guests. Most often, breakfast is set up with an accessible coffee station and a buffet with cereals, fruit, muffins, and yogurt. Custom egg orders or a breakfast special prepared by the chef usually follow later in the morning. Lunch can be served via a buffet, family style or individually, while dinner is typically served individually. It all depends on the level of service on the boat.

<u>First course</u> ~ to continue with the order of course placement, set the starter on the charger, and at the conclusion of the meal, remove the charger with the salad plate, if it is in fact not a proper charger but a dinner plate. Or, you may leave a proper charger down through the entire meal, and pull it with the final course before dessert.

During the first course, check the wine and water glasses. If a guest has carried a wine glass to the table that is the same wine being served at the meal and has finished it or is depleted enough for you to refill it, remove it entirely, and simply fill the fresh wine glass that is part of the place setting. Also refill any bread plates, and inform the chef how slowly or quickly they are eating—and, of course, relay any compliments!

<u>Meal complaint</u> ~ one of the most important things to remember about serving the food on a yacht is that the chef has strategically planned for every meal. It is vital that you not volunteer any food that you have seen in the galley or volunteer the chef's services in whipping up a special request. Cooking is *not* your domain; do not create confusion

by suggesting anything that the chef has not given you permission to offer. Now, if a guest refuses his mixed green salad, let's say because he only eats romaine, kindly remove it. At this point, you can both ask if he would like something else and say that you will see if the chef has romaine available. Go to the galley and relay the events to the chef. Let him figure out a solution.

Tip: ⚓

Have a garbage bin available in the galley, out of the chef's working area, so you can dispose of food and stack the plates off to the side until there is time and room to wash them.

Before the next course, make another quiet pass around the table, and remove any utensils or condiments that will no longer be required. This is proper and also leaves less to do later. Of course, pour more water and wine, as long as you're not overbearing about it! Topping off too often is bothersome.

Serve the main course on top of the proper charger, and as you place the first plate, announce the dish one time with the chef's description. For instance, you might say "Asiago-encrusted sea bass with wasabi mashed potatoes." You do not need to announce the broccoli or beans or anything obvious. Keep it short, and be sure to say it loudly enough so everyone at the table can hear you.

Tip: ⚓

Will the guests need a fingertip bowl or warm, moist towel after their lobster dinner? If you believe they will need to wash their hands after a course, be sure to provide a moist towelette or fingertip bowl. If you fail to do this, they will get up from the table, go down to their rooms, and throw off the timing for dessert service for the chef. Suddenly, guests find themselves in their rooms, and venture into checking cell phone messages and freshening makeup! You can prevent this insanity (and give great service) by rolling and moistening a towelette for each person in advance in warm, lemony water (don't squeeze the lemon over them directly, or it will leave yellow streaks and spots). Set them on a tray in the microwave or oven and carefully keep them warm. Serve with tongs and stand close by, because you will have to collect them almost as soon as you pass them out.

Tip: ⚓

Some guests smoke after their meal—will they need an ashtray during dessert? Have a clean one available. If the men present cigars, be sure to have a proper torch lighter and cigar-sized ashtray.

Notify the chef when you will begin clearing the main course. As you clear each place, be sure to take the charger and any utensils that were set for *that* course with you. Before you leave each place, reach up to the dessert utensils and slide them down to the right side of the placemat. Aren't you glad you clear from the right, so you can easily accomplish this task? Also, locate the salt and pepper, and any other condiments that were used during the course, and remove them as well. The table should be cleared of everything that is no longer required for the next course.

After the table is cleared, notify the chef that the table is ready for dessert, then return to your guests and offer an aperitif or coffee or tea. If the chef is ready for you to serve dessert, by all means, serve it. If the chef is not ready, you can begin delivering the guests' beverage selection to the table. I never ask if a guest wants dessert. Simply serve it. This minimizes interruption and preserves the chef's hard work invested in preparing it.

Before serving coffee and tea, make an effort to place the cream and sweeteners on the table. This way guests can prepare their coffee or tea immediately upon receiving their cup.

Some guests may linger well after the meal has concluded and other guests have left the table. Clear all of the dishes and empty glasses and coffee cups. Do not remove the placemats unless they are blowing away in the breeze or are offered to you. You do not want to stop a conversation inadvertently while trying to pull a mat out from under someone's elbows!

Tip: ⚓

Be sure to learn how to use the espresso and/or cappuccino machine well before a guest requests a cup. Check to see if it needs to be turned on in advance to heat for example, so that there is less delay in your service.

EXTRA GUEST SERVICE

Extra services can make for a great trip and make you look like a genius! Consider preparing for the following, and have a blast being a star!

1. Know the weather—you will be asked to be a meteorologist. (Don't say I didn't warn you!)
2. Know the ETA to destinations.
3. Gather local information about the area you're visiting to share with guests (anything to get them off the boat!) Just kidding!
4. Learn the audio-visual system in all guest areas.
5. Have board games, DVDs, cards, and anything else to entertain on a rainy day.
6. Arrive on deck with icy-cold cloths guests can use to cool the skin.
7. Prepare a DVD with photos and music to help them remember their trip.
8. Prepare a book for each stateroom, illustrating safety procedures, directions to operate the TV and stereo, and some interesting facts about the yacht and the crew.
9. Try serving the latest trends in anything! Trendy magazines can lead you in fascinating directions!
   Beer and chocolate tasting
   Wine tasting
   Vodka taste test
10. Perhaps your current location is known for its:

    Clam chowder
    Saltwater taffy
    Exotic fruit

This is great entertainment and incredible bonus fun for guests—they're on vacation, after all. Even if it's their fifteenth weekend on their own yacht, you can turn it up a notch!

A DAY AT THE BEACH

It will be your responsibility to prepare some items for the guests' day at the beach. Pack a large bag with a towel for each person and a cooler with drinks and snacks.

Consider keeping a bag on the tender with a supply of sun block and headache and seasickness medicine. The tender should have a first aid kit and flares, too.

EVENING TURNDOWN

Preparing a stateroom for the evening can be quick, once you do it a time or two. Start by setting out a chilled bottle of water and a chocolate for each guest in case you are interrupted—at least they will have the essentials!

1. Place water in a carafe on the sideboard or by the bedside.
2. Place a chocolate on the turndown corner of the bed sheet or by the bedside.
3. Insert blackout discs in portholes.
4. Pull the shades.
5. Turn down the bedspread and stow, if possible—otherwise, fold in accordion fashion so they can simply pull it up to their chin should they get cold during the night.
6. Stow all decorative pillows.
7. Fold the top sheet and blanket down from the entry corner.
8. Iron pillowcases.
9. Set the sleeping pillow in an upright position by grabbing the top corners of the case.
10. Dry towels and return to correct rooms.
11. Empty the trash bin.
12. Fold toilet paper.
13. Wipe down all surfaces.
14. Dry the shower by scraping with a squeegee and drying with a chamois cloth.
15. Vacuum, if required.
16. Adjust lighting to an evening glow.
17. Perhaps turn on some soft music.

Be consistent, turn down the same way every evening.

Anticipating a guest's needs is always appreciated. If you have a guest who is subject to seasickness and your vessel will be underway tomorrow, leave some medicine on their vanity. If they are partying up a storm, leave them two waters and aspirin!

LAUNDRY—the untamable beast!

Firstly, laundry requires power and water. Make sure that you check the availability of both with your captain, especially while at anchor. Beyond that, the most important thing to remember is that laundry can be difficult to keep up with. Imagine cleaning the uniforms of ten crew members who wear two different uniforms each day, the linen napkins from luncheon and dinner, the galley dish towels, the rags used to clean the exterior, the beach towels, and guest items—oh, and it's the third day of the trip, so you have the sheets from every guest cabin as well. The point of the story is to keep up with it. Get in the habit of constantly turning it over so you can fold and iron when you find the time and avoid being buried. The machines are small and delightfully over-engineered to have very long cycles, but there will probably be at least two washers and dryers on board, so it is, however, manageable.

Laundry Supplies— You will need:
Detergent
Fabric softener
Bleach pen
Stain remover
Iron
Ironing board
Spray starch
Spray bottle for water while ironing those tough wrinkles

Tip: ⚓
Large containers of laundry soap can be unwieldy. Use these to replenish smaller bottles that are easier to stow and manage.

Ironing can be difficult, as it is only on larger yachts that you will have a large ironing board available to you. Consider hand-pressing items and folding sheets properly while they are still damp. Also, do not hesitate to iron sheets as you are making the bed.

Tip: ⚓

The trick to folding fitted sheets is to tuck one end of the pockets into the other. This will leave you with a gathered edge on top, gathered sides and a straight edge on the bottom. Lay the sheet on a flat surface and neatly establish the top and sides. Fold one side over on top of the other, so the gathered edges are on top of one another. This keeps the gathered areas from unnecessarily wrinkling the smoother areas. Then fold the rest of the way, first beginning with the gathered edges. This will result in a smooth tidy package.

Remember *not* to run laundry in the evening in the guest area because of the noise and the potential end-of-cycle signal. Also, do not run them while you are underway, because the motion of the vessel can damage the machine, especially while it's in a spin cycle. While at anchor and underway, the yacht is making fresh water and is powered by generator which provides a limited amount of power. Therefore, as mentioned previously, it is important that you verify with the captain that there is enough power and water to run washers and dryers.

Hopefully you will exercise ethics in sorting the laundry into loads. For instance, wash the galley towels in their own exclusive load on hot. Dark items like towels should never be combined with light items. The lint is virtually impossible to remove, and will make both items look dingy. Also, do not be tempted to fill out that puny load of dinner napkins with your bra and panties!

Tip: ⚓

You can save yourself excessive laundering of guest towels by drying them only. Toss them in the dryer while you are cleaning their stateroom, and return them to the same stateroom shortly afterward. On the third day of a trip however, all heads should be replenished with fresh clean towels.

Tip: ⚓

Use color coded safety pins to help you identify the owner of laundered articles. Small beads or colored thread can be attached to the pins, and then pinned into the garment.

Tip: ⚓

Empty the lint screen before every load. Clean it often with soap and water if you use a fabric softener, as it tends to clog the pores in the screen.

PURCHASING—Yes! You get to go shopping!

Typically, the chef will purchase the garnish, snacks and drinks your guests need; just hand them the list, and they'll incorporate it into their own provisioning. You, however, will be in charge of purchasing specific things like flowers, specialty items like welcome gifts, seasonal mementos, and soft goods for the vessel. Maybe the boat is to begin chartering and the vessel now requires a new separate set of linens for guests, beach chairs for a barbecue, umbrellas, coolers, and souvenir hats. The list of what you may find you require for a yacht is endless.

Consider:

Linens	DVDs	Table Decorations	Wine Pull
Towels	CDs	Beach Towels	Cocktail Shaker
Cooler	Beach Chairs	Beach Umbrellas	Napkin Rings
Throws	Bedside Trays	Serving Trays	Cream & Sugar Set
Slippers	Robes	Placemats	Beach Table
Candles	Hurricanes	Medication	Crew Uniforms

Customized items are a big trend, for every owner enjoys seeing his yacht's name stylishly adorning personal items.

Hats & Visors	Towels	Linens	T-Shirts	Water Bottles	Stationery
Can Cozies	Door Mats	Pillows	Beach Towels	Hand Towels	Bath Products
Picture Frames	To-go Cups	Crystal	Silver Trays	Slippers	Napkin Rings

When purchasing the more durable items for the boat, it is wise to let quality and material dictate your decisions. As the saying goes, 'the bitter taste of bad quality lingers longer than the sweet taste of a good deal.' Within reason, choose items that will clean easily, wear well and require the least maintenance.

Placemats: All cotton and bright colors will look faded after a few washings. Consider mats made of materials that are partially made with a synthetic that will wash well, hold its color but release the stains. Some nice plastic and vinyl styles will wipe clean easily.

Bed linens: The label may say that the thread count is 1000, but is it high quality Egyptian cotton? Sometimes higher thread count is *not* an indicator of quality, and you may find the sheets pill after only a few washings. Do not be tempted to purchase discount sheets online for instance, stick with known brands.

Dishware: Chefs love white! White plates and bowls are the perfect stage to plate their beautiful food. White also makes it easy to incorporate colors when setting the table, improvise with colored accent dishes and they are easy to replace.

Tip: ⚓

Take special care to measure the width and depth of the cabinets and drawers before purchasing chargers, dinner plates and glassware. It can be an unwelcome surprise to find that they don't fit. Make note also of the width of the cabinet at the top, because even if one plate fits, the entire stack may not. If you plan on washing them in the dishwasher, be sure they fit in there too!

Service pieces: Have fun with these. There are dozens of super stores that offer inexpensive platters, bowls and trays. Buy two or three of each so that they can be used at the same time to set a cohesive buffet. Be sure to buy small bowls too that can be used to hold dips and sauces.

Glassware: Will it fit in the dishwasher? The cabinet? Is it top heavy? Thin and breakable? Is it versatile, can it be used for different beverages and to serve food, say, to hold a soup or dessert?

Beach towels: Buy white! Self tanner, suntan oil, new swimsuits and food can wreak havoc on the beach towels. These stains will show on colored towels too, I assure you. White however, does not fade or collect bits of lint and can easily be refreshed with bleach. Monogrammed names are not in danger of being harmed, as the thread used in the stitching is typically resistant to bleach.

FLOWERS, FLOWERS EVERYWHERE!

Ordering flowers, especially in places unknown to you, can be a daunting task. If you have the time, take a taxi to the shop and speak with the florist in person. This way, you will get what you want. I suggest you consider the following:

1. How many arrangements do you need to order? One for the aft deck table? The dining room table? The master suite? The sky lounge?
2. How many single stems do you need to order? A grouping for the day head? Each stateroom? For the chef to use for plate decoration?
3. Style of arrangement—do you want a tropical look? Romantic? Formal? Masculine?
4. How hardy must it be? Will it be outside? Inside? In gale-force wind?
5. What colors are preferred? Reds and yellows? Monochromatic?
6. What size arrangement would you like? Will guests be able to see each other across the table? Will it interfere with the table setting?

If you do not know the names of flowers, ask that the yacht buy a book. If you do not know what type of arrangements you or the owner likes, ask that the yacht buy a book. Once you achieve a look you like, keep photos and notes so you can repeat it in the future. Maybe, hmm, keep them in the book!

Artificial flowers have come a long way since the days of old Aunt Mabel and her purple roses in the bathroom. I encourage you to consider having a store of reasonably convincing artificial stems to use if you are ever somewhere so remote that fresh is out of the question. I suggest tall reeds, grasses, and tropical blossoms, as these tend to look the most realistic. Steer well clear of roses, mums, and carnations. Any flower that it is common is easier to be detected as artificial!

STOWING THE VESSEL TO TRAVEL

Stowing the boat is vital to protect the interior accessories. While guests are on board, stowing is not typically that involved, as yachts rarely travel when the seas are large enough to upset the interior or make guests uncomfortable. If the seas are rough you will hopefully not be leaving the dock.

In any case you may have a few things to secure just to be certain. Removable gels are very effective gum adhesives that will keep most objects secure on most surfaces. If however, you have a towering floral arrangement and feel this size is beyond the capabilities of this gel, place the arrangement on the floor against a sturdy cabinet or by the back of a sofa and brace it with chairs or other heavy object. You may find that some of the *objets d'art* may already be permanently secured with an adhesive named 5200. If it has been secured with 5200, it is never coming off and you do not therefore need to worry about it.

Rolls of rubber non-skid mats are available at grocery stores and marine stores and are effective under anything that may slide; the toaster and the candy basket! This mat is also used to line shelves all over the boat, including staterooms, bathrooms, and the galley. You can also use pieces of it to cushion anything you might stack—like plates, for instance. Felt pads are available too, and should be used between plates of fine china to protect the delicate finish.

Take a walk through every room on the vessel *before* and *during* your time underway, and check for items that may get tossed with the waves. It is important to ensure that cabinets and drawers have not opened, and that shower and closet doors are not swinging wildly on their hinges. Stow loose items in drawers and cabinets or as a last resort, line the sink or tub with a towel and wrap the items with additional towels. Close the lid of each head—anything other than toilet paper and what one consumes can do untold damage to the head system!

Stow the boat while it's calm, because once the seas start rolling, you will not have time to secure everything, nor will you be as effective when doing so. Working while it is rough is also how you can get hurt, it's easy to lose your balance and fall into something or slip on the stairs. Also, while you are underway, especially in heavy seas, it is very important that you be available to assist the captain and mate in vessel safety. You may be asked to keep watch from the helm or on the tow, and you do not want to be distracted by things crashing around in the interior! It will break your heart to have to pack up a vessel you've worked so hard to bring up to your standard of organization. Suddenly, all of your neatly folded towels are crammed into cabinets! This is why they pay you, of course, but it always made me think, "ughhhh."

Owners and guests virtually never travel with the yacht when it relocates to a new destination. Thus, you may not have as many little accoutrements to stow. But, because they are not on board, keep in mind that you may encounter much bigger seas while underway. Use everything at your disposal to keep things from rolling around inside the cabinets. You can stuff towels into drawers, rolls of paper towels into cabinets, and tape off entire banks of drawers and shower doors with a non-marking blue tape. Lay down the dining room chairs and the barstools in the lounge; anything that is top-heavy can easily be tossed by the sea.

Tip: ⚓
Ask the captain or the mate how big he expects the sea to be.

NOTES

CHAPTER 10

ORGANIZING YOUR TASKS

The following is a general outline to give you an idea how your day may unfold. You may find your day beginning at 4:30 AM and ending at 8:00 PM, every boat is different. You will develop your own system of organization after a week or two of trips with guests. If you are a highly organized person already and are able to anticipate what is required from you during every point of the day, you don't need this outline. Lucky you!

6:30AM   Start the coffee
Pre-boil the water for tea, so it will not take as long to heat when a guest actually wants it
Set the breakfast table
Set up the coffee station
Set up the breakfast buffet
Wipe down or dust any interior surfaces
Straighten the salon, lounge, and other common areas
Clean the day head
Set out deck accoutrements i.e. towels, flowers, chairs, cushions, amenities
Iron the napkins from the day before
Continue any laundry

Tip: ⚓
Ask the mate to go out and purchase a selection of the daily newspapers.

8:00AM   Guest Service

If you have set a coffee station, guests will help themselves and probably venture on deck to read the paper or a book and enjoy the view. Typically, the chef will have you serve fruit platters, cereals and such while waiting for other guests to rise. Once all have seated themselves, a breakfast special or eggs to order may be offered. You might want to have a piece of paper handy to record the orders; this way the chef will have the precise information, and you can move on to other demands—for instance, a guest may request you run down to their cabin to check on their spouse who doesn't feel well, and deliver a ginger ale. Truly, you will find yourself being pulled in a myriad of directions.

	Serve the breakfast
	Replenish the coffee and creamer, etc.
	Clear the table
	Load the dishwasher
	Continue any laundry

9:30AM — Stateroom Service
Dry any damp towels and return them to the room from which they came
Make the beds (change the sheets after the third night)
Raise any sunshades
Wipe and dry the shower, sink, and reflective surfaces
Wipe clean the floor
Shake the bathroom rug, or use a lint brush to remove any debris
Clean the toilet and close the lid
Fold the toilet paper; replenish it if it is low
Remove any garbage
Straighten the vanity
Replace or replenish any vanity items
Vacuum
Dust all surfaces
Straighten the room

11:00AM — Prep for the Afternoon
Set the table for lunch one hour before service is to begin
Locate any service pieces the chef may require
Ensure wine is chilled and glasses are clean
Check the drink refrigerators and replenish
If the guests are off the yacht, vacuum the public areas
Check windows and doors for fingerprints
Continue any laundry and ironing

12:00PM — Guests Return to the Yacht
Stand on deck for greeting

Offer to assist with packages, etc.

Have towels available for guests who may have been out in the water

Announce when (or again, confirm with the hostess when) lunch will be served

Take any drink orders

12:30PM   Lunch Service

Fill glasses with ice just prior to seating guests

Take any requests for drinks

Serve the meal

Standby for any requests

Clear the table and assist with galley clean up

1:45PM   Be available on deck to serve guests

Prepare sun bed or lounge chairs

Straighten salon and other common areas

Continue any laundry and ironing

3:00PM   Evening Prep (already?..yes!)

Discuss the service pieces and plating requirements for dinner with the chef

Pull coffee service pieces, and place them out of the way so you may access them

Pull the plates, napkins, platters, and utensils for hors d'oeuvres

Set out nuts or bar mix on the bar

Set up the bar

Ensure wine openers, mixing spoons, and shakers, etc. are available

Check the staterooms for wet towels or rumpled beds, as some may have come in from a day on the water or taken a nap

Cut any fruit or garnish for cocktails

Ensure wine is chilled and chilling for the evening meal

5:00PM   Cocktail Hour

Serve any hors d'oeuvres the chef may have prepared

Replenish ice buckets, lemons and limes
Decant any red wine that will be served with dinner
Fold the napkins for dinner

6:00PM   Dinner Prep
Set the table for dinner
Pull all of the required service pieces

7:00PM   Dinner Service (prior to guests being seated)
Light candles
Ice the water glasses and fill them with water
Place butter on the table
Brew coffee

7:15PM   Dinner Service
Notify the chef when the guests are being seated
Present and pour the wine
Clear any empty cocktail glasses, or offer to replenish
Serve the appetizer and any bread that may
accompany this course
Replenish beverages

Update the chef on the guests' progress through the first course—and relay any compliments, of course!

Slowly remove plates as guests finish. Leave the plate of a guest (even if it is empty) next to any guest who is still eating; this way they will not feel rushed.

Check the progress of the next course with the chef—he or she may need more time. If this is the case, you can slow the pace with which you clear the table.

Ensure that the coffee has brewed, and that hot water is available for tea

Prepare a tray with teas, sweetener and cream to be taken to the table

8:00PM   Prior to Dessert Service
Remove all utensils and condiments that were part of
dinner service

Ensure all guests have the proper utensils for dessert
placed on their right
Replenish beverages
Place coffee and tea cups at each place setting
Place sweetener and cream on the table

8:15PM   Dessert Service
Serve coffee and tea
Serve dessert

If you are on a small yacht as the only stewardess you may at this point choose to either return to the galley and assist the chef with clean up or hand off the remaining table service to another crew member and begin stateroom turndowns.

8:30PM   Stateroom Turndowns
Finish one room before you begin servicing another
First check the towels for dampness and begin drying
them in the dryer
Replace any dirty towels with clean ones
Pull the window/porthole shades
Turndown the beds and stow the spread and pillows
Iron the top sheet and pillow cases to present a crisp look!
Furnish each guest with water and a chocolate
Dry the shower, tub and the sink
Shine all surfaces
Straighten the vanity
Clean the toilet and close the lid
Replenish the tissue, the toilet paper and vanity supplies
Fold the toilet tissue
Shake out the bathroom rug
Wipe down the tile floor with a slightly damp cloth
Remove the garbage
Retrieve the dry towels from the dryer and replace
Dim the lights in the stateroom and head to an
evening glow

9:30PM   Check on the guests
Rotate any laundry

Assist in the galley

10:00PM   Check on the guests
Straighten the outside decks
Clean the dining table
Replenish drink refrigerators
Stow crystal, china, silverware and all service pieces
Set up the morning coffee service in the galley

10:30PM   Check on the guests
Rotate laundry
Iron the napkins etc.
Pull the service pieces for the morning meal

11:00PM   Straighten the salon
Wipe clean all surfaces
Remove any fingerprints

11:30PM   Night, night, termite!

NOTES

_____

_____

_____

_____

_____

_____

_____

_____

_____

_____

_____

_____

CHAPTER 11

WHAT THE OWNERS WANT YOU TO KNOW

INTERACTION

You must obviously interact with guests and owners in order to be effective in your job. Only you can determine the extent of your interaction based on their service needs and their receptivity to you. Pay attention, and you will gain a sense of how to interact with all of them very quickly. Adhere to the following, and you won't go wrong:

1. Ask questions at opportune times.
2. Never sit while having a conversation with a guest.
3. Keep your side of the conversation brief until you learn how interested they really are in what you have to say.
4. Never comment, laugh, or anything else when you overhear a conversation between guests.

SERVICE

The owners want you to know that they care more about their guests than themselves. Meet the needs of a guest equally as well as you would for an owner, and you will be loved by your owner! Be consistent in your frequency of service. If they can count on you to at least be consistent, they aren't left wondering when you are going to show up again.

THEIR YACHT

Yep! It's their yacht. It's easy to lose sight of this when you live and work on the vessel full time. You will establish your way of doing things, and they may want to change them.

For instance, you may establish a system for tying up lines with the captain, and then they want to participate, making your job more difficult. Let them do it! If they want to have dinner up top on the fly bridge and you've already set up for the meal on the aft deck, smile and change it! They may want to participate in mixing drinks, thus slowing you down, but let them do it! It's all about them; remember that you have been hired to facilitate their enjoyment of their yacht. Making them happy makes you a great stewardess.

ETHICS

Do the right thing! You must exercise ethics in every aspect of your job. Do not steal, do not cheat, and do not lie. The owner has entrusted you to protect his investment—do not become a liability. Think ahead! If it's raining outside and you have workmen or guests boarding soon, pull out towels, extra doormats, and carpet runners (if necessary), and be ready to help dry things off. If you are entrusted with a credit card, keep meticulous records of your spending, and write the description of and the reason for the purchase on the receipt. Otherwise, during accounting at month's end, if you are questioned about what you bought, the answer may be a distant memory.

TAKE SOME TIME OFF!

Owners are, for the most part, kind and understanding. They will embrace you like family and truly care about your happiness and well-being. They may implore you to "not work so hard" or "take some time off of the boat." These sentiments are well-intended, but be sure to remain consistent in your service. More than likely, if you are offered the chance to go ashore, it will be for only an hour or two during the day. My guess is because you are new in this industry; you will be too tired to take advantage of the opportunity. But, if you do choose to go, carefully think through your obligations to the vessel and the guests. Although they may be encouraging you to explore for a while, even the keenest of owners does not understand how much work and preparation time you need to do your job well. You may find yourself returning to the boat happy and relaxed, and find them looking at you wondering why they haven't been served a cocktail!

NOTES

CHAPTER 12

HOW TO SET UP A BAR—The ten drinks you should know!

It is very helpful to have a bartender's mixing guide, but you can also find different recipes for drinks on the Web sites of most liquor brands, as well as on food and wine Web sites. These are the most requested mixed drinks that require any knowledge—we'll assume you know what is in a rum and Coke!

*1. **Margarita**—mixers abound which enable you to simply salt the rim and add tequila and a lime wedge. You can blend this drink and serve it frozen, or add sweetener to appeal to any palate. Salt the rim!*

> *1 ½ oz. tequila*
> *1 ½ oz. Triple Sec*
> *1 oz. Rose's Lime Juice*
> *½ juiced lime*

Rub the rim of a glass with lime wedge, dip in salt. Shake with ice and strain into glass. Garnish with a lime wedge.

*2. **Martini**—traditionally, gin is the primary ingredient in a martini, but the latest fad is vodka.*

> ***Gin martini** (Dry) This is 5:1 ratio*
> *1 2/3 oz. gin*
> *1/3 oz. dry vermouth*

Shake or stir ingredients over ice, strain into chilled martini glass, and serve with choice of olives, onions, or lemon twist!

Vodka martini
> *1 2/3 oz. vodka*
> *1/3 oz. dry vermouth*

Keep in mind that most people simply want vodka shaken over ice and strained into a martini glass with their choice of garnish, so do not hesitate to clarify the ingredients.

*3. **Bushwacker**—this can also be a frozen, coffee-flavored, island-style cocktail! Use coffee ice cream in place the cream and blend with ice cubes.*

> *½ oz. coffee liqueur, like Frangelico*
> *½ oz. amaretto*
> *½ oz. light rum*
> *½ oz. Irish cream liqueur*
> *2 oz. light cream*

Blend and pour over ice.

*4. **Planter's Punch**—a refreshing, rum-based drink that makes one think of the islands!*

> *juice of 1 lime*
> *juice of ½ lemon*
> *juice of ½ orange*
> *1 tsp. pineapple juice*
> *2 oz. light rum*
>
> *1 oz. Jamaican rum*
> *2 dashes Triple Sec*
> *1 dash Grenadine*

Combine first five ingredients over ice and shake vigorously. Pour over ice in collins glass and add Jamaican rum. Stir. Top with triple sec and grenadine. Decorate with slices of fruit or a cherry.

*5. **Daiquiri**—a versatile rum drink—once you know the foundation, you can improvise and add fruit to make your own version, i.e. pineapple, peach, mango, coconut, or strawberry!*

> *juice of 1 lime*
> *1 tsp. powdered sugar*
> *1½ oz. light rum*
> *1C. fruit nectar of choice*

Shake, stir, or crush in a blender

6. **Cosmopolitan**
>¼ C. Cranberry Juice
>¼ oz Rose's lime juice
>¼ oz citron vodka
>¼ oz Triple Sec or Cointreau

Shake vigorously with ice and serve up in a chilled martini glass with a twist of lemon peel.

7. **Vodka Collins**—*you can substitute whiskey, and you'll have a whiskey Collins. If you eliminate the club soda and cut the sugar in half, you'll have vodka sour or whiskey sour, depending on what liquor you use.*

>*juice of ½ lemon*
>*1 tsp. powdered sugar*
>*2 oz. vodka*
>*club soda*

Shake first three ingredients with ice, strain into tall glass, and add ice and club soda. Garnish with lemon, orange, and cherry. Serve with a straw.

8. **Hurricane**—*a Mardis Gras favorite*

>*1 oz. dark rum*
>*1 oz. light rum*
>*1 tsp. passion fruit syrup*
>*2 tsp. lime juice*

Shake with ice and pour over ice into a tall glass.

9. **Bloody Mary**—*a terrific "morning after" drink. Many versions of this classic exist; some even seem to turn the drink into a salad by garnishing it with rolls of salami, marinated green beans, olives, and marinated onions! To spice it up, add horseradish or wasabi powder. To lighten it up, you can add an ounce or two of clam juice. You can treat the rim of the glass*

by moistening it with a lemon wedge and then dipping the rim in Old Bay seasoning. Serve with a celery stalk… if you have the room!

Classic Bloody Mary

> *1 ½ oz. vodka or pepper vodka*
> *3 oz. tomato juice*
> *½ lemon, juiced*
> *½ tsp. Worcestershire sauce*
> *2-3 drops of Tabasco*
> *Salt and pepper to taste*

Shake with ice and strain over ice cubes into an old-fashioned glass.

Bull Shot

> *1½ oz. vodka or pepper vodka*
> *3 oz. chilled beef bouillon*
> *1 dash Worcestershire sauce*
> *1 dash salt and pepper*

Shake with ice and strain over ice cubes into an old-fashioned glass.

10. **Pina Colada**—*frozen, creamy goodness that always sets an island mood!*

> *3 oz. light rum or coconut rum*
> *3 tbsp. coconut milk*
> *3 tbsp. crushed pineapple or pineapple juice*

Combine in blender with ice and strain into a festive glass. Serve with a straw, a pineapple wedge and a cherry.

SETTING UP THE BAR

Setting up a bar is necessary, whether or not the guests will be serving themselves. You will need to have a selection of liquor, wine, mixers, sodas, and garnishes. These may include:

Lemon wedges	Horseradish	Olives
Lime wedges	Celery	Celery salt
Pepper	Marinated green beans	Old Bay seasoning
Worcestershire	Marinated onions	Margarita salt
Hot sauce	Orange wedges	Stuffed olives
Cream of coconut	Crushed pineapple	Wasabi paste

Equipment you may need:

Martini shaker	Stirrers	Wine bucket
Blender	Sharp knife	Ice bucket
Long spoon	Cutting board	Ice scoop
Cocktail napkins	Straws	Wine opener
Bottle opener	Bar towels	Wine vacuum
Wire Strainer	Stirrers	

Tip: ⚓

When chilling wine and champagne in ice, wrap the entire bottle in plastic wrap or a plastic bag to protect the label.

Tip: ⚓

The favored way to cut bar lemons and limes is to slice off both ends to the flesh, then set it up on one end and slice into wedges lengthwise. Use your knife to remove the membrane from the innermost part of each wedge. This should leave you with a clean, meaty wedge with no seeds.

NOTES

CHAPTER 13

SAVE THE DAY WITH YOUR COOKING! —Two easy solutions for each meal of the day.

If you lose your chef, and you weren't crazy about him or her anyway, you may consider yourself lucky. Soon, though, it will sink in that you have to cook until a replacement can be found! Well, it may not happen, but it could! Whether it does or not, you may find an opportunity to cook for crew and find that you enjoy it. Keep in mind that many smaller yachts employ cook/stews, so start practicing!

Breakfast

You can fold virtually anything into scrambled eggs—try veggies, bacon, or smoked salmon. This is my personal favorite!

CRABBY EGGS—serves four
8 eggs, lightly beaten
1/3 block cream cheese, diced into small pieces
4 oz. lump crabmeat
Chives, diced for garnish

Slowly heat the eggs in a skillet over medium heat. Fold them over gently as you go. When the eggs are partially cooked, fold in the cream cheese and crabmeat. Be careful not to break up the nice lumps of meat. Turn onto a plate, and sprinkle with chive and paprika.

PINA COLADA PANCAKES—serves four to six
2 cups Bisquick
2 eggs, lightly beaten
4 tbsp. Coco Lopez
2 tsp. vanilla or 2 tsp. Kahlua
¾ cup milk

Blend all ingredients together, leaving some lumps. Pour into a well-oiled, hot skillet. When bubbles form around the edges of the pancake, flip and finish cooking another minute or two. Garnish with a browned pineapple ring, sliced bananas, and toasted, diced coconut sprinkled on top.

Syrup: mix equal parts Coco Lopez and maple syrup.

Lunch

Anything goes for lunch!

TOASTED SANDWICHES—serves four
8 slices any bread (the more rustic, the better)
8 slices provolone cheese
Assorted slices of meat, salami, turkey, proscuitto
16 basil leaves
Custom Spread (follows)

Make a simple sandwich spread by combining cream cheese and herbs such as basil, thyme, and tarragon with a bit of Dijon mustard, garlic, and sun-dried tomatoes. Process until smooth.

Assemble sandwiches, lightly oil the outside of the bread slices, and toast in a dry, hot skillet, pressing down with another skillet to make them brown and crunchy.

CHOP CHOP SALAD—*this is an "everything" salad and is always a hit. It's useful because any ingredients on hand can be used; however, it can also be time-consuming.*

Assorted greens, iceberg and romaine are good choices
Tomatoes, seeded and diced
Onion, diced
Cucumber, seeded and diced
Olives, seeded and diced
Bacon, cooked, drained and diced
Egg, hard boiled, peeled and diced
Cheese, diced (feta, bleu, any will do!)
Corn kernels, drained
Chicken, cooked and diced

Finely chop (1/4 inch dice) the greens, make a bed on a plate; then layer the ingredients of your choice in decorative stripes over the top, or in sections radiating out from the center. Serve assorted dressings on the side.

Hors D'oeuvres

Super-easy and fun to experiment with!

CROSTINI WITH TAPENADE—*do not be intimidated! You do not need all of these ingredients for this spread to be a success!*

1/2 lb. brine-cured black olives, such as Gaeta, Vall'Aurea, or Nicoise, pitted
2 anchovy filets, drained
2 tbsp. capers, drained
2 tbsp. chopped fresh parsley leaves
1 tbsp. fresh lemon juice
1 tsp. minced garlic
1 tsp. grated lemon zest
1/2 tsp. fresh thyme leaves
1/4 tsp. freshly ground black pepper
6 tbsp. extra virgin olive oil

In a food processor, combine all ingredients except olive oil. Process slightly and scrape down sides of food processor. With the motor running, add the oil through the feed tube, and process to a smooth paste, scraping down sides as needed. Adjust the seasoning to taste.

Lightly oil and toast slices of small bread, preferably baguette. Spread onto the toasts and serve with a sprinkle of herbs.

NUTTY CHEESE SPREAD

12 oz. cream cheese, softened
1 tsp. Worcestershire sauce
3 tbsp. Liquid Smoke
4 oz. sharp cheddar cheese, finely grated
¼ cup each of celery and bell peppers, finely chopped

1/3 cup pecans, finely chopped
2 tbsp. onions, minced
dash Tabasco sauce
½ tsp. garlic powder

Mix everything except pecans. Chill several hours or overnight. Spread the chopped pecans on waxed paper and roll the cheese ball through them until coated. Chill completely before serving. Serve on a base of hot pepper jelly or other fruit jelly with assorted crackers.

Dinner

Dinner can be as easy as lunch if you play it right!

SWEET AND SOUR SHRIMP—*shrimp cook quickly, so it's perfect if you have little time.*

¼ cup chicken stock or water
3 tbsp. ketchup
3 tbsp. sugar
3 tbsp. pineapple or orange juice
2 tbsp. vinegar
2 tsp. soy sauce
3/4 tsp. crushed red pepper flakes

2 teaspoons cornstarch (dissolve in 2 tbsp. of stock and set aside)

1 lb. shrimp, peeled, with tails intact
2 tsp. minced ginger
2 tsp. minced garlic

2 tbsp. peanut or vegetable oil
1 cup thinly sliced onions
1 cup 1-inch chunks green bell pepper
1 cup pineapple chunks
12 maraschino cherries
6 tbsp. thinly sliced green onions

Hot white rice (accompaniment)

To make the sauce, combine 1/4 cup stock, the ketchup, sugar, juice, vinegar, soy sauce, and 1/2 teaspoon of the pepper flakes in a bowl. Set aside.

In a bowl, toss the shrimp with ginger, garlic, and remaining 1/4 tsp. pepper flakes. Set aside for 10 to 20 minutes.

Heat a large wok over high heat. Add the oil, swirling to coat the sides and bottom of the pan. Add the shrimp, garlic, and ginger, and stir-fry until pink, about 2 minutes. Remove from the pan.

Add the onions and peppers, and stir-fry until tender-crisp, about 2 minutes. Add the sauce and cook, stirring, until the sugar dissolves. Add the cornstarch mixture and bring to a boil. Return the shrimp to the pan and add the pineapples, cherries, and green onions. Cook until the sauce is thick, about 1 minute.

Remove from heat and serve over rice.

MEDITERRANEAN PASTA

3 tbsp. olive oil
1 lb. skinless, boneless chicken breasts, sliced diagonally

1 (8 1/2-oz.) jar sun-dried tomatoes, julienned (1 cup)
2 tbsp. garlic, minced
1 lb. fresh angel hair pasta
1/4 cup fresh basil
1 (8 1/2-ounce) can artichoke hearts in water, quartered and drained (1 cup)
1/2 cup kalamata olives, pitted (1/4 pound)
6 oz. feta cheese, crumbled
1/4 cup heavy cream
2 tsp. dried oregano
salt and pepper to taste

Boil water for pasta in a pasta pot fitted with a strainer. Heat oil in a skillet over medium heat. Brown chicken strips until no longer pink (about 3 minutes each side). Add sun-dried tomatoes and garlic to skillet. Sauté for 2 minutes. In the meantime, add the fresh pasta to boiling water, and cook until al dente, about 5 minutes.

Now add the basil, artichoke hearts, olives, and feta cheese to the skillet. Sauté 1 minute, then stir in the cream. Strain the pasta and transfer to a large pasta bowl. Add the chicken sauté to the pasta and toss. Season with oregano, salt, and pepper before serving.

Dessert

Even fresh fruit marinated in rum and sugar is a great dessert!

CARAMELIZED PEACHES

1 (29 oz.) can peach halves in heavy syrup
½ cup heavy cream
1 tbsp. cognac
1 tbsp. fresh lemon juice

Heat the syrup for 10 minutes over high heat to reduce the liquid. Shake the pan near the end as it turns a deep golden color. Add peaches and stir in the heavy cream. Boil for 1 or 2 minutes, and then transfer to bowl. Allow to cool, then stir in the cognac or brandy and the lemon juice. Add 1-2 tbsp. water if the syrup is too thick. Cover and refrigerate until serving time.

You can serve this over ice cream or over leftover cake pieces toasted under a broiler. Top with the peaches and sauce and sprinkle with pistachios.

ROYAL MOCHA FREEZE

1 pint whipping cream
5.5-oz. can chocolate syrup
1/3 cup brandy
1 quart coffee ice cream, softened

1 6-oz. pkg. semisweet chocolate morsels
3/4 cup almonds, toasted

Combine the first three ingredients and fold into ice cream, stir in well, then rest and freeze uncovered 3 hours. Spoon the ice cream into parfait glasses and garnish with chocolate morsels and almonds. Serves 12.

NOTES

_____

_____

_____

_____

_____

_____

_____

_____

_____

_____

_____

_____

_____

_____

_____

_____

_____

_____

_____

_____

_____

_____

CHAPTER 14

NOTE-KEEPING

> Do you know where to find wine in St. Maarten?
> Flowers in Newport?
> A dry cleaner in Abaco?

If you have the opportunity to arrive at a port a few days before guests arrive, take a walk, or better yet, take a jog around and scope out the area. Are there interesting restaurants? Is there a famous landmark? Are there any special events that will occur while you are moored there? Pick up any available literature so your guests may peruse it once they are on board.

If you run any errands for the boat while you are in port, keep every business card, address, phone number, and contact name. As you gather these tiny bits of information, record them in a book for your future reference. When you go into a store, take note of any unique items they may sell and record this information. You may suddenly be asked by a guest where to find a birthday gift for their spouse, and it's a tremendous help to them when you know a bit about a store or have a number to call to make an inquiry.

Tip: ⚓
Keep this information with you as you change jobs so you can build a library of resources.

Record the birthdays and anniversary of your owners, giving a card or a gift collectively from the crew is a really nice touch.

NOTES

CHAPTER 15

DOWNTIME AND YARDTIME—They are not the same

Downtime is a time without guests on board, and is a welcome time on any yacht, no matter how much you may cruise. This is when the yacht is sitting idle and may not be used for a while. This is the opportunity to "spring clean" the interior and exterior, if this is also your realm.

1. Empty and wipe clean all of the drawers and cabinets —every single one— in the salon, the galley, the staterooms, the bathrooms, the lounge, the bridge, and all other nooks and crannies.
2. Clean and sterilize the refrigerators, wine coolers and ice makers, clean the vents and coils.
3. Clean the oven and the microwave.
4. Clean and sterilize the trash compactor and other trash receptacles.
5. Wash or dry-clean the bedspreads, pillows, and blankets.
6. Details! Clean and sterilize the toilet brush holder, cotton swab the grout etc.
7. Wipe the blinds and vacuum the furniture and the curtains.
8. Check all of your service linens, napkins, and placemats for wear and stains. Spots tend to appear over time, even though they have been clean. Go figure!
9. Polish the silver.
10. Check all of the crystal for dust, fingerprints, and lipstick.
11. Check all air-conditioning filters for dust every two weeks.

Tip: ⚓

The air handler for each room draws a lot of air to cool or heat the room. They are located out of sight, under beds, in closets and behind paneling. Because of their constantly drawing air, lint and dust tend to collect along the edges of drawer and door frames, crevices and the like even though there may be a vented panel to feed the handler.

12. Dispose of any foods that are more than six months old.
13. Dispose of and replace any napkins, serving trays, glasses, etc. that are looking worn.
14. Order those extra pieces that you found you needed during service, i.e. a wine decanter.
15. Schedule professional carpet and furniture cleaning—remember that the interior will not be accessible until the carpet dries, so schedule this toward the end of the day or on a weekend.
16. Restock the yacht with all of the necessary supplies:
    a. Cleaning supplies
    b. Toilet paper and other bathroom items
    c. Soaps and shampoos
    d. Vacuum cleaner bags
    e. Laundry supplies
    f. Bar supplies
    g. Beach supplies
    h. Galley supplies like sponges, compactor bags, soap, foil, and wrap

When the boat goes to the "yard," it is usually for a number of general maintenance issues or a re-fit. Boat yards are busy, filthy places from which your yacht leaves in worse condition then when it arrived. They are located near interstates and airports. The air is filled with flecks of paint, fumes, and dust. Workmen are sanding and grinding on almost everything. It is a time when you may be given some time off. It is very difficult to accomplish any deep cleaning because of the level of activity and filth on and around your boat.

If your boat is undergoing major refit work inside or out, consider the following: Bag everything! No, I don't mean quit; I mean literally bag everything. Depending on the intensity of the project, you may want to use plastic to protect furniture, mattresses, and entire rooms.

NOTES

CHAPTER 16

DEFINITIONS

Abaft—behind the vessel.

Abeam—beside the vessel.

Aft—toward the stern.

Bosun's Locker—the locker on deck where lines, fenders, and cleaning supplies are usually kept.

Burgee—a flag flown on the bow that usually carries a yacht club logo or an owner's chosen design.

Courtesy Flag—this is flown on the starboard side mast or starboard side spreader on a sailboat. It is the colors of the country in which you are currently visiting.

EPIRB—Emergency Position Indicating Radio Beacon. An onboard beacon mounted outside on the bridge that will transmit your vessel's position to the coast guard in the event of sinking.

Fly Bridge—the highest station, outside, from which the vessel can be driven.

Fore—forward toward the bow.

Galley—the kitchen.

Heads and Beds—this is a slang term used by people in the industry to denote the work of a stewardess. "Heads" stands for bathrooms, and "Beds" stands for the beds in the staterooms.

Helm station—any point from which the vessel can be driven.

Lazzarette—the aftermost hold of the vessel located aft of the engine room, and usually accessed from the swim platform.

Lines 1, 2, 3, 4—typically line 1 is your bow line, working toward the stern, which is line 4. This is a technique used by captains to simplify communicating which lines will be passed to or from the dock in which order.

Pilot House—the raised, interior, area from which the vessel is driven.

Runners—carpet covers that offer protection from soil and water. They attach with snaps and metal grommets to the floor. They are used primarily when only crew and workmen are on board.

Spring Lines—these are lines used to tie the vessel to the dock. They typically are secured to cleats that are located along the side of the vessel and extend toward the bow and toward the stern when they are tied off to the dock. They prevent the vessel from moving forward and backward in its slip.

Starboard—the right side of the vessel when facing the bow while on board.

Stars and Bars—this is slang for the formal epaulet shirt that serves as uniform for crew.

Swim Platform—the aftermost deck, close to the water. This is used to board small water craft and tenders, and provides easy access to the water.

STCW—the international convention for the Standards of Training, Certification and Watchkeeping for Seafarers, or the Seafarers Training Certification and Watchkeeper's Code. This is a basic firefighting, water survival, and vessel safety course that will ensure your awareness of certain procedures and techniques.

Team—two crew members who come to the job as a pair.

Tender—the small boat a yacht carries to use for exploring and accessing shore.

T/T—the label before the name on the yacht's tender. It stands for "tender to."

VIP—the secondary stateroom, usually slightly smaller than the master stateroom.

Watch Keeping—the rotation between crew to monitor driving or anchoring conditions.

NOTES

_____

_____

_____

_____

_____

_____

_____

_____

_____

_____

_____

_____

_____

_____

_____

_____

_____

_____

_____

_____

_____

CHAPTER 17

VESSEL SAFETY—You must be aware of the following aspects of safety!

Muster Station— This is a predetermined place for all guests and crew to gather to evacuate the vessel.

Life Jackets— There should be a life jacket for every passenger on board the vessel. They are typically stowed under outdoor seating or in outdoor lockers for quick access. Find them!

Station Bill— A station bill outlines the obligations of each crew member to the guests and the vessel in the event of an emergency. It is posted in the crew area. This is the best way to coordinate the efforts of crew members and prevent duplicate efforts and oversights.

Life Raft— The U.S. Coast Guard states this is the number one life-saving device; it keeps the body dry and warm, and provides a large, visual target. These rafts are mounted on the outside decks of the vessel, and are rigged with a hydrostatic device that will automatically release the raft in the event the vessel sinks. It is also possible to manually release the raft, and the instructions are pictured on the container.

Ditch Bag— A ditch bag is prepared in advance of a trip; every captain should have one, but you should also have your own if you will often be offshore. This is a waterproof bag that will hold anything you care to have with you, should you find yourself stranded at sea without a vessel. You may choose to pack a VHF radio, strobe light, food bars, water, flares, matches, sunglasses, sun block, and a hat.

EPIRB— The EPIRB (Emergency Position Indicating Radio Beacon) is mounted on the uppermost deck of almost any vessel, and is used to help the coast guard locate the vessel in the event of sinking. It emits a radio frequency automatically. It should float free and come to the surface if you are unable to grab it before you leave the ship. Find it and hold on to it! After all, you want the coast guard to find you, not the boat!

VHS Radio All vessels are required to monitor channel 16. This channel is used to communicate with other boats, bridges and shore.

Fire Extinguisher— Locate all available fire extinguishers, read how to use them, and frequently check that they are fully charged. If you are the first one to a fire, yell "FIRE!" while you work to extinguish it and until you are assisted. Additionally, pounding of the boat while underway will cause the components to settle in the canister, so check their charge every three or four months.

Galley Blanket— This is a fireproof blanket stowed within easy reach of the stove, which is used to extinguish grease fires. This is preferable to a canister extinguisher, as it is less likely to chase the flames up the exhaust chute into the ceiling of the vessel and will not contaminate food.

Longitude and latitude— These are the geographical points on a chart that identify your specific position on the planet Earth. These numbers are on the GPS at the bridge, and will look something like the following: 018 26' .50" N   064 45' .80" E. Knowing where to locate this **very valuable and specific** information on the bridge and how to identify it will greatly assist a search team.

Mayday Call— Hailing "Mayday" on VHF radio channel 16 is the universal call of distress. The proper procedure for a mayday call is "Mayday, Mayday, Mayday, this is the motor yacht/sailing yacht _____call letters _____. Our location is (Longitude) (Latitude)." State the nature of the emergency, the number of passengers on board, any injuries and any additional pertinent information.

NOTES

CHAPTER 18

THE JONES ACT—your rights as a crew member

The Jones Act is a United States Federal statute that was enacted in 1920. Its operative is found at 46 U.S.C. 688 (a), which provides:

"That any seaman who shall suffer personal injury in the course of his employment may, at his election, maintain an action for damages at law, with the right to trial by jury, and in such action all statues of the United States modifying or extending the common-law right or remedy in cases of personal injury to railway employees shall apply."

This act extends to sailors the Federal Employers Liability Act, also known as FILA. It entitles sailors to what the Act calls "transportation, wages, maintenance, and cure." This means the employer or ship owner must get an injured sailor home, pay wages while he's unable to work, and provide medical care for his injuries until the sailor has recovered to his fullest extent. If the sailor was injured due to negligence by the employer, captain, or another crew member, the sailor may be able to obtain damages for pain and suffering from the employer or ship owner.

Indeed this act offers some assistance in the event that you are injured. However, it does not replace the need for you to purchase your own health and/or injury policy to ensure your well being.

NOTES

CHAPTER 19

ASSESSING YOUR GOALS IN THE YACHTING INDUSTRY

There are many things to consider when deciding your future working aboard a yacht. Ideally, you know yourself very well, and know your desires, your limitations, and your goals. To assist you in exploring your reasons for pursuing any career, I encourage you to address the following statements.

Answer the first set of questions BEFORE you move to the next set, and you may discover some very important things about yourself.

First, record your three major goals by working in this industry:

1.

2.

3.

Now record three circumstances in which you would not be content:

1.

2.

3.

And the best part, list the three ultimate circumstances that could happen for you in this industry:

1.

2.

3.

Focus on your goals to determine the steps you must take to be successful. Never accept a position that will put you in a situation you see as an absolute negative. And hold true to the belief that you can attain your "ultimate three" and beyond. I know this to be true, because what is your dream is someone else's vague interest. You may want to see the world, while another may prefer to travel only one week a month. So voice your desires to your agent(s) and in your interviews, because their needs may equal your dreams.

NOTES

_____

_____

_____

_____

_____

_____

_____

_____

_____

_____

CHAPTER 20

YOUR RÉSUMÉ—in search of the right boat.

The most important parts of your résumé for this industry are vastly different from what is emphasized in the business world.

1. List every single job you've held in the yachting industry, no matter how small or how short the time span.
2. List any land-based jobs that you believe will translate well to yachting. For example, management and service experiences are both considered valuable to a vessel.
3. List any jobs you've held that others may find of interest. If you used to be a dive instructor, a piano teacher, or a golf professional, the owner may want you just for the lessons!
4. Include your picture on the first page. This is an image-conscious business, like any hotel or restaurant. Yachts prefer you be clean-cut and fit. Physique sells!
5. State what you are willing to do. This includes travel for long periods of time or care for children, pets, or the elderly.

Additionally include:

1. Citizenship, for only American citizens can work on an American-flagged vessel
2. Willingness to travel
3. Hobbies and interests
4. References—list names and numbers that a potential employer may contact. Be sure to inform your references that you are seeking employment and confirm that they are willing to speak on your behalf.

NOTES

CHAPTER 21

PREPARING FOR A JOB INTERVIEW—first impressions and ex-spouses last forever

You will find that most crew around the docks dress in beach shorts, T-shirts, and flip-flops, captains included. This is all well and good and completely accepted. However, do not underestimate the importance of your appearance in an interview. After all, this is a high-profile, high-style industry, and you must convey that you grasp these qualities instantly in your hygiene and dress. Pay attention to the following to ensure you look like the stylish professional that you are!

1. Hair combed and neatly styled
2. Nails clean and trimmed
3. Easy, killer… go lightly on the makeup
4. All clothing should be appropriate for the season—do not wear a white sundress on a winter afternoon, even if it is ninety degrees outside. It is in poor taste, and your interviewer will notice and you may not be hired
5. Arrive fresh, bright, clean, and well ahead of time! If you are running the risk of being late, call your interviewer fifteen minutes before your scheduled time and let them know.

BE SURE NOT TO DO THE FOLLOWING:

1. Do not have anything in your mouth—no gum, no mints, no posts.
2. Do not arrive smelling like a cigarette, even if the job permits smoking.
3. Do not wear a hat or sunglasses.

Dress in smart, casual clothing. A daytime dress is fine with conservative shoes or sandals. Slacks with a button-front top or a smart-looking ensemble are winners. Sleeveless tops are all right, but be sure your bra straps are hidden. Never wear midriff-baring or cleavage-revealing tops. This style is better reserved for the beach or a wild date. Shoes should be conservative, not too high or too sexy, and of course, in good condition. Press your clothes, and go get 'em, tiger!

Jewelry is fine, but please—you're not interviewing to be a Vegas showgirl.

1. No more that one ring on each finger.
2. No more than one earring in each ear.
3. Go lightly on the bangles and beads.
4. Piercings and tattoos are taboo; take them out or cover them up.

Tip: ⚓

If you are nervous and believe you may perspire during the interview, wear a top that will disguise it, or a light sweater or jacket that will hide any underarm wetness.

Tip: ⚓

Drinking lots of icy cold water will lower your body temperature and will actually give you a chill. Drink up, so you walk in cool, calm, and collected, instead of wiping your brow!

QUESTIONS YOU SHOULD BE PREPARED TO ANSWER:

1. Why did you leave your last job?
2. What are your goals?
3. What are your expectations while working on my yacht?
4. What do you expect to be paid?
5. How do you handle stress?
6. What do you think your finest contribution will be?
7. How long do you think you will be happy in this position?
8. Do you get seasick?

Feel free to elaborate when answering questions posed by the interviewer espccially if you feel you are exceptional in some way compared to other people being interviewed for the position. For example, offering that you can assure some level of longevity on a boat can be reassuring to a captain and owner. They do not look forward to having to replace crew members; it is a huge interruption to the smooth operation of the yacht.

QUESTIONS YOU SHOULD BE PREPARED TO ASK:

1. What are the duties of the position?
2. What is the environment of the boat?
3. What are some of the rules for crew?
4. How does the owner use the boat?
5. What is the pay, what is the pay schedule, and how will I be paid?
6. How is vacation time and time off arranged by the captain?
7. Are there any benefits I should consider?
8. Will there be an opportunity to advance?
9. Will there be an opportunity to learn about other positions on board?
10. What is the yacht's itinerary?
11. How long does the owner anticipate owning the yacht? Is it his desire to eventually buy a larger yacht? How long has he been in yachting?

Pay close attention to the body language of the interviewer. Remember that if it is the owner, the captain, or the chief stewardess, you will be working for them. Are they kind, calm, and respectful toward you? Are they rushed, nonchalant, or dismissive toward you? How do they respond to you when you ask questions of them? They, like you, should be looking for the *right* stewardess for their yacht, not just the *next* stewardess for their yacht.

Evaluate the policies of the vessel, the description of your job, and the overall personality of the interviewer. The interview is your best opportunity to find out about the boat, so be very inquisitive and discerning so that you can ensure that you are going to be happy and productive onboard.

NOTES

CHAPTER 22

CREW AGENCIES, BROKERS, AND MANUFACTURERS

There are a number of ways to market yourself in the yachting industry. The most obvious way is through a crew agency, but leaving résumés with people you meet in the business is also highly effective.

Crew agent services are usually free of charge, and they can capably assist you in finding employment on the yacht of your dreams. They will receive a commission based on your salary from the yacht that employs you, and they guarantee your services for at least thirty days or the duration of the contract, if shorter than thirty days. They place crew all over the world and are terrific allies!

Yacht brokers sell, trade and charter boats to buyers. They are typically interested in establishing a crew database as this is a vital component of their business. Recommending qualified crew is a way of facilitating a sale. It relieves the new buyer of now having to take an extraordinary step in using his new yacht.

Many crew and broker agencies have Web sites; this simplifies staying in touch with their stable of crew members, who are spread out all over the world. These agencies can be found by searching online, in yacht magazines, and in maritime newspapers. Register with as many crew agent and broker Web sites as you choose. Upload your résumé (which some call a CV, *curriculum vitae*), upload your picture, your references, your certificates (STCW or Dive Master, for example), and fill out their online interview. Then, and only then, will they let you make an appointment to meet you in person. Keep in mind that they will not promote you until they've met you in person and contacted your references.

Once you are registered, most ask that you check into their Web site at least once a week to remain on their "hot" list of those seeking immediate employment. While visiting their website you can review the available jobs and submit your interest. Signing with as many agents as possible is expected, and it increases your odds of finding the right agent and the right job. Do not underestimate the power of developing a great relationship with your agents! As they get to know you, they can more accurately place you on a yacht that fits your personality.

There are websites that are hosted by crew members for crew members, where you may post your résumé and job search specifications. You can also post a classified ad online with some of the more prominent maritime newspapers that cater to captains and crews. Typically, all of these services are free.

Another highly effective way to promote yourself as a crew member is networking. Take advantage of any opportunity to befriend fellow crew, as a majority of jobs are acquired via word of mouth. Consider attending crew social functions, boat shows, classes at a maritime institute and even 'crew night' at certain bars. Making friends can be as easy as walking the docks and striking up a conversation. Try it!

Befriending vendors in yachting can lead to employment also, as captains and owners often inquire if these industry folks know of any crew available for hire. Uniform companies, bookstores, canvas makers, interior yacht design companies, marine supply stores etcetera, are valuable allies when you are looking for a job.

NOTES

_____

_____

_____

_____

_____

_____

_____

_____

_____

_____

_____

CHAPTER 23

EXPANDING YOUR MARKETABILITY

You can expand your marketability in many ways. There are many stewardesses who offer more than service skills on board, and are paid accordingly for their multiplicity. These additional skills include:

1. Massage therapist
2. Yoga instructor
3. Dive instructor
4. Nanny
5. Nurse
6. Chef
7. Personal assistant
8. Personal shopper
9. Helicopter pilot
10. Airplane pilot
11. Nutritionist
12. Bartender
13. Florist
14. Interior designer
15. Sommelier
16. Multi-lingual

There are a number of courses you can take that will certify you in some way within a week or two. These courses are offered at area colleges, universities and art and maritime institutes. Sometimes an owner will pay for this additional education. It is worth feeling them out!

NOTES

CHAPTER 24

ADVANCING YOUR CAREER

Chief Stew
There are opportunities to advance your career in yachting as a stewardess. The chief stew position is available on every mega-yacht in the world, and carries with it a great deal of responsibility and financial reward. If it is your interest to move up the ladder into a chief stewardess roll, by all means, go find work on the biggest boat that will hire you. The best way to secure a lucrative career on a mega-yacht is to work your way up on a mega-yacht.

Chef/Stew
If you find that you want to expand your responsibilities on board but remain on smaller boats with fewer crew, consider culinary classes, and begin cooking and cleaning! If you can balance the workload, it can be fun. Be forewarned! This combination of positions is highly demanding, and is best reserved for casual service yachts with an owner with an understanding of the demands on you and who has reasonable expectations.

Captain
If you would like to be a licensed captain or mate in the future, consider taking courses at a maritime institute or even a naval academy. The most important things to secure in your pursuit of your captain's license are sea time, helm experience, and knowledge of navigation, systems, and engineering. Beyond the courses, take a position on a yacht as a deckhand, or even as a stew/mate on a small yacht, and let the captain train you. Experience is the best teacher.

Broker/Estate Manager
Land-based jobs abound after a career on the water. As mentioned, the yachting industry is a friendly business based on networking. The knowledge you acquire and the friends that you make may lead to interesting avenues like yacht broker, charter broker, personal assistant and estate management just to name a few.

<u>Crew Agent</u>

Crew agents are matchmakers of a sort. The ability to decipher personalities and match crew with yachts is a terrific skill. Many crew agents were formerly crew members, so if you have an interest in moving to a land-based job, but do not want to leave yachting entirely, consider a job at a placement agency.

NOTES

_____

_____

_____

_____

_____

_____

_____

_____

_____

_____

_____

_____

_____

_____

_____

_____

_____

_____

_____

_____

CHAPTER 25

ASSESSING A JOB OFFER

Assessing different opportunities on different yachts requires some insight and experience. In the beginning of your career, you probably will not have many options from which to choose. But, while you are boat hopping, take note of the tangible and intangible benefits of the different yachts on which you work or from your conversations with other crew, so you gain more insight into this industry. The following spreadsheet can guide you through a comparison of jobs on different boats and help you determine your value to a boat, thus the salary you deserve.

Hers is how it works. Assign a value to each category, depending upon what each particular boat offers. If you have an actual dollar number in mind, by all means enter it, but for cells that are based on your particular desires (for example, *geography*), I recommend you use a scale of $1,000-5,000. This will keep you on track, and produce a more accurate picture. Work your way down the spreadsheet, and fill in all of the spaces that apply to that particular yacht.

Tangible benefits are the remunerations you receive for doing your job. Here are some examples of what is indicated by the cells in the spreadsheet.

Charter Gratuity—Is the boat a charter boat? What can you expect to earn in tips each year? Fill in the estimated amount in the appropriate square.

Education—Will the boat pay for your continuing education, such as culinary classes, which will help you advance your career?

Additional Benefits—Does the owner have his own plane and invite you to travel on it? Does he own a professional sports team and give you tickets? Can you use the tender to play on your day off? Assign a value between $1,000 and $5,000, depending on how valuable the additional benefits are to you.

Intangible benefits are those benefits that are personal to you and your situation. Consider the following aspects of a position and their value to you.

Experience—Will the experience you gain by working on board greatly enhance your career and your marketability in the industry? Will you be solely responsible for the interior, or will you gain tremendous knowledge by working under an experienced chief stew?

Enjoyable Work Environment—Do you have your own cabin or your own head? Do you like the other crew members? What is the lifestyle on board for the crew when guests are and are not on board? Can you smoke? Drink? Have friends over?

Number of Guests—How many guests will typically be on board? Are there enough crew to provide consistent quality service and provide rest for the crew?

Balance of Time Off—Is the captain considerate and reasonable about offering you days off after long trips?

Geographic Base—Is the boat based in an area that you enjoy?

Itinerary— What are the ports of call? What is the duration of the itinerary? How frequent are the trips? How far from home will you be traveling? Is the boat planning to circumnavigate the globe? Is this attractive to you, or are you a homebody? If the itinerary for an 80-foot yacht is to travel to the Caribbean, a 110-foot yacht to the Mediterranean and a 180-foot yacht to New England and your dream is to go to the Med, you will put a larger positive value in the cell for the 110-foot.

Benefits to owner are the qualities that you as an individual bring to the job. How you compare to other people is a significant aspect of any job interview. By grasping your own value to a yacht, you can interview with greater self confidence and poise. Yachting is an image conscious business. Your appearance, demeanor, professionalism, and personality will be given considerable weight. Use these qualities to your advantage. For instance, if the owner is a high profile CO and often entertains, he will most assuredly want a crew member who will represent him well.

Experience— What knowledge, skills and experiences do you embody that are of benefit to the owner? Do you have charter experience? Hotel management skills? If the owner habitually receives massages for instance and you are a massage therapist, you will be viewed very favorably for hire. Place a value in the cell that represents your skill level and its value to the owner.

Education— Are you a college graduate? Are you a world traveler or one who has lived abroad? Are you multi-lingual? Hiring keen crew may be important to the owners' image and enjoyment. If level of education is important to the owner, place a value between $1,000 and $5,000 in the cell based on the level of education that you bring to the operation in comparison to other crew members.

Presence and Personality— Do you enhance the onboard experience because of your persona? Are you enjoyable, lighthearted and fun while maintaining a professional level of service? Some owners want to embrace their crew like family while some want very little interaction. If you consider yourself the type of crew member the owner is looking to hire you will place a positive value in this cell. If you feel this is not an important characteristic to consider, leave the cell blank.

Longevity— Are you able to offer the owner a certain degree of longevity? Perhaps you are interested in the itinerary of the yacht, the size of the operatin or even the location of the yacht's home base. Place a value in the cll to represent the degree to which ongevity is imporant to te owe

	80' YACHT	110' YACHT	180' YACHT	INDUSTRY STD.
Tangible Benefits				
Base Salary				
401(k) Match				
Insurance - Life				
Major Medical				
Dental				
Eye				

Education				
Charter Gratuity				
Cellular Telephone				
Computer				
Internet access				
Company Car				
Vacation				
Travel Benefits				
Education				
Christmas Bonus				
Additional Benefits				
Intangible Benefits				
Work Environment				
Enjoyable Geography				
Itinerary				
Experience				
Total Value to You				
Benefits to Owner				
Level of Experience				
Education				
Presence and Personality				
Longevity				
Total Assessed Value				

NOTES

CHAPTER 26

NEGOTIATING THE TERMS OF YOUR EMPLOYMENT

<u>Current Salary Guidelines</u>

You should clarify the following before you accept a fulltime position on a yacht:

1. Salary
2. Vacation Time
3. Job Description

<u>Salary</u>

The best place to begin your salary negotiation is to download the current day rate and salary guidelines from several of the crew agencies online. Search for yacht crew agencies online, or thumb through boating magazines and maritime newspapers for agency advertisements. These guidelines will help you determine the average pay level for any position on different-sized vessels. Caution—they do not necessarily keep them current, so use your head, and check out more than one Web site. Remember, too, that day rates are usually higher than a salaried position. The assumption is that a salaried position is receiving additional benefits.

Pay is dependent on experience (DOE). You may have to start at the bottom of the pay scale, but you can always negotiate for an increase in pay, say, after sixty or ninety days. It is up to you to determine your worth and be brave enough to ask these things up front of an interviewer. If they will not even entertain the idea of increasing your pay after evaluating your performance, I would question how pleasant it would be to work for them.

To negotiate your salary or ask for a raise, write a letter to the captain and owner outlining your qualifications, experience, and licensing. If you offer a combination of skills above the industry standard, you should be rewarded for your talents. State what amount you are asking of them.

Vacation Time

In the United States, it is typical to receive two weeks of paid vacation a year. Confirm the amount of vacation you will receive and the procedure for arranging the time off. It is also important to ask if the yacht will repatriate you to your home port to begin your vacation if it happens to be in a different locale. Remember, holidays typically belong to the owner! Try to schedule your vacation time well in advance so there is no conflict.

Job Description

It is very important that you clarify the scope of any position you accept. You may be hired as the stewardess, and find out that you are now also the crew cook. You may be hired as the mate, and then be expected to be the stewardess and make the beds. Well, needless to say, these types of surprises can be taxing and upsetting. If you find yourself in an interview wondering who will be responsible for certain tasks, by all means, ask the interviewer. If you find you are handling two jobs when you were under the impression you were hired for only one, bring it calmly and without emotion, to the attention of the captain or owner. Offer your ideas for a solution.

NOTES

_____

_____

_____

_____

_____

_____

_____

_____

_____

_____

_____

To order additional copies of *What Every New Yacht Stewardess Should Know,* please visit us online at yachtstewardess.com.

Lightning Source UK Ltd.
Milton Keynes UK
171254UK00001B/16/A